Praise for *Who Are Your Best People?*

"Every chapter of this book is filled wit. ....on sense that, as the authors explain comprehensively, is unfortunately not that common in how organizations manage people. If you want to improve your business behaviours you can do no better than by reading this book."

Peter Swinburn, President and CEO Molson Coors

"This book solves the HR manager's dilemma about what gift to give to the CEO. It's the most useful, practical and sensible book on talent management in print today."

Colin Patey, Senior Vice-President, Global, Interhealth Canada

"What Messrs, Stuart-Kotze and Dunn don't know about talent management could be written on the back of a very small performance appraisal form."

Paul Bumpstead, Managing Director, Reinsurance, HSBC Insurance Brokers Limited

"If your organization doesn't have a Talent Management Programme in place, read this book, and if it has already developed one, read it twice."

Saud N. Al-Omair, Al Faisaliah Group, Saudi Arabia

"If you don't see your people as a major competitive advantage, you need to read this book."

Nick Inkster, CEO SSP UK (Air) and Western Europe

"Effective talent management is the key to superior corporate performance, and no serious manager should go without this superb and practical guide."

Alan Yu, Vice-President and Chief Operating Officer, CK Life Sciences International (Holdings) Inc., Hong Kong

"In an environment as changing as China today talent management has become a top priority for corporations. This book comes at exactly the right time."

Benoit D. G. AMS, author of Doing Business in China, a Practical Approach

"We've been waiting a long time for a really practical book about how to manage talent. This is it."

Helen Kelly, International Editor, The Working Manager, USA

"This book will help organizational leaders develop strategies that can pay off in developing their critical resource – people. Readers can expect a controversial and challenging take on existing dogma of talent management."

Dr Robert Rosenfeld, CEO, Centre for Organizational Excellence

"This book is easy to read and it makes a lot of sense. The concept of defining talent as the people whose performance behaviours match the behaviours required in the job, not only makes a lot of sense, but is also really practical."

Dr Filbert Cheung, Director, Asia Training and Consultancy Company Limited

Who Are Your Best People?

FT Prentice Hall
FINANCIAL TIMES

In an increasingly competitive world, we believe it's quality of thinking that gives you the edge – an idea that opens new doors, a technique that solves a problem, or an insight that simply makes sense of it all. The more you know, the smarter and faster you can go.

That's why we work with the best minds in business and finance to bring cutting-edge thinking and best learning practice to a global market.

Under a range of leading imprints, including *Financial Times Prentice Hall*, we create world-class print publications and electronic products bringing our readers knowledge, skills and understanding, which can be applied whether studying or at work.

To find out more about Pearson Education publications, or tell us about the books you'd like to find, you can visit us at **www.pearsoned.co.uk**

PEARSON
Education

Who Are Your Best People?

How to find, measure and manage
your top talent

Robin Stuart-Kotze and Chris Dunn

Prentice Hall
FINANCIAL TIMES

An imprint of **Pearson Education**

Harlow, England • London • New York • Boston • San Francisco • Toronto • Sydney • Singapore • Hong Kong
Tokyo • Seoul • Taipei • New Delhi • Cape Town • Madrid • Mexico City • Amsterdam • Munich • Paris • Milan

Pearson Education Limited

Edinburgh Gate
Harlow CM20 2JE
Tel: +44 (0)1279 623623
Fax: +44 (0)1279 431059
Website: www.pearsoned.co.uk

First published in Great Britain in 2008

© Pearson Education 2008

The right of Robin Stuart-Kotze to be identified as author of this work has been asserted by him in accordance with the Copyright, Designs and Patents Act 1988.

ISBN: 978-0-273-71522-1

British Library Cataloguing-in-Publication Data
A catalogue record for this book is available from the British Library

Library of Congress Cataloging-in-Publication Data

Stuart-Kotze, Robin.
  Who are your best people? : how to find, measure and manage your top talent / Robin Stuart-Kotze and Chris Dunn.
      p. cm.
  Includes bibliographical references and index.
  ISBN 978-0-273-71522-1 (pbk. : alk. paper) 1. Personnel management.
2. Employees--Recruiting. 3. Job satisfaction. I. Dunn, Chris. II.
Title.
  HF5549.S89443 2008
  658.3--dc22
                    2008034097

10 9 8 7 6 5 4 3 2 1
12 11 10 09 08

Typeset in 9/13pt Stone Serif by 30
Printed by Ashford Colour Press Ltd., Gosport

The Publishers' policy is to use paper manufactured from sustainable forests.

To three people who exemplified Best and whom I miss greatly:

Peter Cole
Graham Cole
Jason Taggart

RS-K

To three people who also exemplified Best, whom I miss greatly and to whom I owe so much. The work you started continues...

Mike Stafford
Margaret Legum
Sir Rowland Whitehead

CBD

Contents

Foreword

It is a rare experience for me to read a book where I have an overwhelming urge to shout 'yes!' to almost every page. But that is what this book does to me.

Why?

There are lots of reasons. The book is well written. It offers lots of real-life examples and case studies. It makes fuzzy things – like what we mean by talent – crystal clear. It challenges some unhelpful myths and assumptions – for example, that talent is in short supply. It has lists of useful questions and things to do … and so on.

But, the *real* reason, of course, is that I'm hopelessly biased! Reading this book is a joyous experience for me because its messages exactly accord with my own values and beliefs. For example:

- That people's performance is the result of their behaviour.
- That behaviour is observable and therefore measurable.
- That people's behaviour is determined more by situational factors than by their personality.
- That organizations/managers have an uncanny knack of stifling people's performance.
- That there is a specific set of behaviours that will produce optimal performance in every job.

It should be clear from this list that I am a behaviourist, in other words I have an unshakeable belief that, no matter how complicated we are, ultimately it is our behaviour (what we say and do) that has an impact. This is not to deny the influence of a whole host of other factors such as underlying thoughts, perceptions, motives, attitudes and feelings. But they are all covert, lurking unseen inside us. In just the same way that your brain, lurking inside your skull, can only have an impact through muscular activity, it is *always* your overt behaviour that makes a difference (for better or worse!) to the world around you.

Some people – you may be among them – find this emphasis on behaviour rather insulting. They argue that, rather like an iceberg with only one-tenth showing above the surface, their behaviour is but a fraction of who they really are. But this misses the point. The bald truth is that it doesn't matter who you think you are; as far as anything 'out there' is concerned – you *are* your behaviour!

One of the strong recommendations in this book is that you should produce precise lists of the specific behaviours that are necessary to produce a high level of performance in a given job. In essence, the idea is to replace traditional job descriptions, 'out of date as soon as they are produced', with job *behaviour* specifications. Once the key behaviours have been identified and described, people can be matched to the demands of the job – preferably though a process that allows for self-nomination (an intriguing approach also described in the book).

This emphasis on overt behaviour has a number of advantages. First, the act of articulating behaviours forces people to be specific about their expectations. Everyone has expectations about how their colleagues and bosses should behave but too often they are left unspoken and implicit. I have always found it very useful to have an 'expectation swapping session' with new starters. I ask them to describe what behaviours they want from me as their boss and vice versa. Understanding at the outset the extent to which, for example, someone expects to be guided, as opposed to being left to get on with it, makes a vast difference to how to get the best out of them. Everyone has a right to know what is expected of them. Spelling it out saves time, removes unhelpful ambiguity, and gives people the information they need to make informed decisions about whether the behaviours that are expected of them are reasonable and in line with their value system.

Second, describing required behaviours puts the emphasis where it should be, namely, on what it is people are required to do to perform effectively. Organizations recruit people for their behaviour, since, as we have seen, behaviour is the only way that human beings can make a difference. Performance is the direct result of behaviours which people have either already acquired or can learn. Merely describing behaviours will not of course get them to happen, but it at least sends out a clear message about the vital role behaviour has to play. Organizations that believe that simply describing the behaviours they want will, as if by magic, get them to happen are in some sort of 'cloud cuckoo land'. A list of desirable behaviours is innocent; it is the use to which it is put that determines the impact.

Third, a clear list of approved behaviours provides the starting point (but I readily admit, only the starting point) for all sorts of sensible actions that would either not otherwise happen, or might happen in an uncoordinated, piecemeal fashion. When behaviours are taken seriously, they infiltrate everything to do with performance management. Key processes such as recruitment and selection, appraisal and coaching, training and development, and even, dare I say it, performance-related pay, are all aligned to the required behaviours. Suddenly a strategic approach to performance management is possible where required behaviours are consistently encouraged, recognized and rewarded.

'Joined-up' behaviourism is powerful stuff. It is cosmetic behaviourism, where behaviours are merely bandied around and issued to staff in glossy booklets, that trivializes the whole business. Worse – cosmetic behaviourism fuels cynicism, as people inevitably contrast what actually happens with the oh-so tidy descriptions of what should happen.

Often people don't behave as we would wish them to, not because they don't want to (though undoubtedly that sometimes is the case) but because they don't know how to. Descriptions of behaviour, providing they are specific, come to the rescue every time. Take, for example, the behaviour, tried and tested, of minimizing the length of a meeting; do it with everyone standing up. Or of maximizing the likelihood of securing someone's agreement; build on what they say. Or of getting someone to be expansive; ask an open-ended question and nod your head while it is being answered. Or of getting people to contribute ideas; ask for them (8 times out of 10 this is successful even with the most reticent person).

So, I unreservedly commend this book to you. But don't just read it; *do it* so that your behaviour helps to create the conditions where everyone is a best performer. The inescapable truth is that behaviour breeds behaviour.

Dr Peter Honey
March 2008

Introduction

All of us do not have equal talents, but all of us should have an equal opportunity to develop our talents.

John F. Kennedy

Before you begin to read this book, would you take a minute or two to write down the names of the five most talented people in your company.

Why did you choose these five people? What makes each of them special? How did you define talent?

According to research at Harvard, talent management is the number one concern of top-level executives at global companies. To be able to take advantage of changing and growing markets, organizations have to have good people in place. And that implies that they know how to identify, manage, develop, keep and get the best out of them. This book is about how to recognize when people are doing a great job, how to measure what they're doing so it can be benchmarked and replicated by their successors when they move, how to help people grow and develop their skills and abilities, how to identify people's potential, how to utilize that potential to its maximum, how to attract people with the right skills and potential, and how to keep them. It's about identifying, recruiting, developing and retaining people with ability (current skill and behaviour) and *cap*ability (future potential). The bottom-line result of doing these things effectively is improved and sustained organizational effectiveness. Managing talent effectively results in increased return on equity, lower cost, higher margins and higher net income.

But before we go any further, we want to make one point clear: *there is no shortage of talented people, there's a shortage of people who know how to identify, develop, recruit and retain talent.* We hope this book will help to rectify this shortage.

The structure of the book

A great deal has been written and said about talent management. It has become one of the buzz phrases of twenty-first-century business. When it becomes difficult to pick up a management journal or to scan a rack of business books without bumping into something about talent and managing talent, one begins to wonder if this is yet another fad that will go the way of quality circles, zero-based budgeting, competencies, just-in-time scheduling, CSR, etc., all of which have added real value to organizations but which have tended to become overused and tired and have lost their cutting edge.

Chapter 1 asks the question 'Is managing talent important?' and quotes research that very clearly establishes that it translates into higher earnings, higher net margins, higher ROA and ROE, and greater competitive edge. Talent management is a serious business; it's not something to be treated as a passing fad. However, as the chapter points out, one of the first problems that discussions of talent and talent management run up against is the word itself. What *is* talent? How do organizations define talent? Because of its varied meanings, interpretations and connotations, instead of talking about talent, we use the word 'Best', and define Best individuals as those people whose behaviour matches the behaviour demands of their job – i.e. they do the things that produce excellent (Best) performance. The analogy is gymnastics: In gymnastics you get points if you *do* some things, and lose points if you *don't do* some things. A Best gymnastics score is 10. That implies that the individual did all the required things for a perfect result.

In Chapter 2 we move on to the issue of how to identify Best people. We made the point earlier on that there is no shortage of Best people; you just have to know who they are. There is a unique and specific set of behaviours that will produce optimal performance in every job, and Best occurs when the individual's behaviour matches the behaviour demands of the job. Therefore Best can only be defined in terms of the job itself.

Chapter 3 moves on to talk about how people can be developed to become Best, and a number of approaches and techniques are described. Chapter 4 addresses a critical issue facing every organization – how to keep Best people. This is as much a problem during periods of slowdown and recession as it is in periods of high growth. The so-called War for Talent began to be trumpeted at the turn of the century and its rationale was strongly based on exploding economic growth in both the Western world and Asia. But a downturn such as 2008 places much more strain on companies to keep their Best people, especially if they're not sure who they are. Although it's in a different context, Chapter 5 describes how to deal with the problem and to keep the Best people while downsizing a number of jobs.

Chapter 6 looks at how to recruit Best people. There are lots of capable people out there who have the potential to be Best, but of course you have to be able to recognize who they are. The TV show *The Apprentice*, with Donald Trump in the US and Sir Alan Sugar in the UK, tackles this problem by putting candidates through a series of tasks, evaluating how they manage them, and weeding out the unsuccessful ones over a period of 14 weeks. But that's TV entertainment. In Chapter 6 we look at how this is done rather more quickly and successfully in the real world. Chapter 7 looks at the issue from the side of the individual rather than the organization and talks about how to manage the transition from one job to another, one company to another and one career to another.

While it's important to know how to identify, develop, keep and recruit Best people, it's equally important to understand what *not* to do. Chapter 8, 'How to kill talent', looks at the things individuals and organizations do to lose Best people and to prevent people from being able to become Best and make a significant contribution. Managing people to get the best out of them isn't easy. The analogy of navigating through a minefield is not far off. Chapter 8 provides a rudimentary map to help you avoid some of the fatal mistakes.

Chapter 9 takes some initial steps towards implementing a system for creating and managing Best people. It sets out some of the important criteria for an effective talent management system. And the final chapter takes a step back from the detail of how to and discusses some of the fundamental issues around managing Best. It's easy to get immersed in the detail; managing talent is critically important for organizational success and it deserves thought as well as action.

Much deserved thanks

A number of people have been extremely generous to us, sharing their thoughts and experience with us and giving freely of their time. Bill Kuhn, our American colleague, is at the top of the list. He's kindly written a short article, which we call *From a Different Angle*, at the end of each of our chapters. He has probably forgotten more about managing talent than most people know. His articles look at the practical application of the concepts discussed in each chapter and give examples of how talent can be managed most effectively.

Chapter 6, 'How can you recruit the Best?' owes huge thanks to Roger Philby and Kevin Howes, both of whom contributed significant pieces. Roger runs a recruitment business called Chemistry and you can tell from the case study he has written that he takes a very different, and highly effective, approach to recruiting Best people. Kevin is a performance consultant who focuses on the issue nearest our hearts – behaviour. His contribution in Chapter 6 is about how to help people entering new jobs make the necessary behaviour changes quickly and effectively.

Karl Chapman is one of those individuals whose work rate and accomplishments are enough to make people who watch him become exhausted. But he very kindly took the time to read the manuscript and his comments were, as always, laser-like and of immense value. We have lost count of the number of times Corinne Hay read various chapters and gave us great feedback. Her patience is astounding. And Rhys Photis, who splits his time between the UK, continental Western Europe and the Middle East, gave us detailed feedback on a number of points. We aren't sure where he was calling from but it sounded as though it was from a very different time zone. Our old friend and colleague, Dr David West, who never fails to help when asked, did his usual startlingly brilliant critique and helped us pull some of our thoughts together. And Alan Yu, as always, put us on track in the early stages of the book. To all of you, our most sincere thanks.

But there are four more people who can take a great deal of credit for the book and who deserve special thanks. At Pearson, Richard Stagg gave us the idea for the book and the title, and Liz Gooster, our wonderful editor, put a huge amount of time into helping us bring out the ideas. And then we have two quite wonderful women who have read the manuscript with fresh eyes and have given us invaluable comments. Coincidentally, they have the misfortune to be our wives. Who said life was fair?

Contacting us

We want all the feedback we can get so here are our email addresses:

rsk@behaviouralscience.com
chris@behaviouralscience.com

The book is a beginning for a very important discussion about talent management, and we have created a website **www.yourbest people.com** for articles, case studies and comment about talent management. We look forward to input from readers.

Robin Stuart-Kotze
Chris Dunn
April 2008

Is managing talent important?

Companies like to promote the idea that employees are their biggest source of competitive advantage. Yet the astonishing reality is that most of them are as unprepared for the challenge of finding, motivating, and retaining capable workers as they were a decade ago.

Matthew Guthridge, Asmus B. Komm and Emily Lawson
McKinsey Quarterly, January 2008

Is managing talent important? No, it's absolutely critical. People really are a company's most important asset. As a manager, what are you doing to uncover and develop the talent in your organization? Do you know who your Best people are? Do you know who your Best people could be? Do your people know what they need to do to be most effective in their jobs? Are they 'engaged'? A Gallup poll in the US found that only 29 percent of workers are engaged, 56 percent are not engaged and 15 percent are actively not engaged, this latter category being defined as 'not just unhappy at work; they're busy acting out their unhappiness. Every day, these workers undermine what their engaged co–workers accomplish.' Similarly, in the UK they found that 20 percent of workers are engaged, 60 percent not engaged and 20 percent are actively disengaged. So only 20 percent of the managers and staff working in organizations can be described as 'working with passion, driving innovation and moving the organization forward, and feeling a proud connection to their company'.

Thinking-intensive versus labour-intensive companies

The world economy is undergoing a fundamental change. For the past 60 years credit has expanded steadily, fuelling increasing levels of consumption. Easy money has made business easy and has papered over the major shortcomings in the way people are managed. Not any more. Research shows that the net income per employee in 'thinking-intensive' companies, where people develop and present ideas, and acquire and share knowledge, is significantly higher than it is in 'labour-intensive' companies, where presumably they are largely ignored. In other words, if you ask people for their ideas, listen to them and encourage them, they tell you very valuable things. Toyota has been doing this for over 40 years and as a result it is the world's largest and most profitable car company.

The concept of labour-intensive companies being any different to thinking-intensive ones is well past its sell-by date. Everyone thinks. Everyone has ideas. Peter Drucker says that if you want to know how to do a job better, ask the person who is doing it. As you do something time and again, you learn how to do it better, faster, easier. But if your boss thinks he or she knows better and doesn't listen to you, why would you bother passing on what you know? The research demonstrating this point, and the opposite when bosses do listen and act on what they learn, is overwhelming. The conclusions are beyond the slightest doubt. But it's often easier to be lazy, and it's easier not to admit that perhaps one doesn't know everything, and it's comforting to feel in control.

There are vast pools of people in so-called labour-intensive organizations, and in *every* organization, who think, who have ideas about how to do things better, who want to be engaged in their work, and who want to be able to make a difference – and whose talents are consistently overlooked. Talent is everywhere. You just have to know how to look for it and how to manage it. That's what this book is about. Having talented people is irrelevant if you don't know who they are, what their talents are, and how to get them strongly engaged, day-in day-out, week-in week-out.

" talent is everywhere. You just have to know how to look for it and how to manage it "

Managing talent and the bottom line

Managing talent well has a huge positive effect on the bottom line. Research carried out by the Hackett Group in 2007 shows that companies that have effective talent management systems, as opposed to those that don't, have earnings that are 15 percent higher, net profit margins that are 22 percent higher, ROA that is 49 percent higher, and ROE that is 27 percent higher.

If that's not enough to convince you, studies done by McKinsey show that companies that have talent management systems and processes that are able to identify two people capable of filling every key job have a 22 percent greater ROE than their competitors. Unfortunately, only about 10 percent of companies do this. No more than a third of all companies have processes that are able to produce at least *one* successor for every key position. The remaining 65 percent flounder around without any defined talent or succession management system.

A recent survey about managing talent in the UK found that 80 percent of the respondent organizations had no formal definition of talent or talent management and only 51 percent of them acknowledged having undertaken any talent management activities.

However, 94 percent of the respondents agreed that if talent was managed effectively, it would have a significant impact on revenue and profit.

In probably the biggest piece of current research on talent management, McKinsey surveyed almost 13,000 senior managers in more than 120 companies and asked them how talent was managed. Many of the results are startling. For instance, managing and improving the talent pool was seen as a top priority by only 26 percent of the respondents. And even more distressing, the research found that virtually no companies made managers at all levels responsible and accountable for developing and retaining talented people. Talent management was seen as the responsibility of 'someone else' – generally some element of HR. However, a paper published in 2006 by the Economist Intelligence Unit in cooperation with DDI begins with the following sentence: 'The management of a company's pool of talent is now too important to be left to the human resources (HR) department alone and has become the responsibility of the top executive.' They draw this conclusion after interviewing 20 corporate leaders from companies with revenues greater than $1 billion. Thirty-five percent of these executives said they spend 30–50 percent of their time on talent management and another 35 percent said they spend about 20 percent of their time on it.

What is talent?

The problem with the word talent is that it carries strong connotations of artistic genius and of innate, genetically determined abilities. It has a hint of showbiz glitz. The vast preponderance of references to talented people are to artists, musicians, performers, athletes, writers or sportspeople. In almost all cases, these individuals are seen as being 'naturals', people who are born with a talent. There is no doubt that genetics plays a significant part in a number of fields. You can't be a top sprinter unless you have fast-twitch muscles, and you can't be a top long–distance runner unless you have slow-twitch muscles. Unless you have excellent hand-eye coordination there are a number of sports at which you will never excel. You can't be a great singer if you're tone deaf and it would be difficult to become a great painter if you were colour blind.

Defining talent

A core issue is how to define talent. *The Economist* says it's brainpower; McKinsey defines it as the sum of a person's abilities; others say 'having the Right Stuff'. Alternatively, it's defined as leadership or emotional intelligence. They all agree on one thing though: they say it's difficult to define or describe talent, but you know it when you see it. Unfortunately, David Hume pointed out 250 years ago that beauty is in the eye of the beholder – i.e. you see what you *want* to see. Therefore 'you know it when you see it' is a purely subjective definition.

What's needed is a more objective definition of talent – one that enables it to be described and measured. The definition we shall adopt in this book is straightforward and free of any jargon. And most importantly it isn't about traits or personality or genes; it's about something you can actually see and measure: *behaviour.*

Talent is the ability and the capability to do something well

Talent has two components: ability (current performance) and capability (potential performance). Ability is about the now; capability is about the future. Both can be observed, tested and measured. Observability and measurability are essential to any objective discussion of talent; if you can't see something and you can't measure it, then how can you be expected to recognize it, let alone evaluate it? Capability requires a bit more effort to observe, test and measure than ability, simply because it involves progressive testing and measurement over time, but it can also be dealt with effectively. We will address this issue later in the book and outline a process that can be used.

> ❝ ability is about the now; capability is about the future ❞

Talent is not just about having the brainpower, the knowledge, the experience, the skill or the mental and physical characteristics to do something currently; it's also about the potential to do something different, or of a higher order of difficulty and complexity *in the future.* Only one side of talent concerns the present. The real payoff is the future: the achievements to which an individual has the potential to rise.

The art of releasing potential

The great virtuoso Yo-Yo Ma began playing the cello at the age of 4 and performed in concert with Leonard Bernstein at the age of 8. His ability was clear at that time but his potential (capability) could only be guessed at. He was not as talented at age 8 as he is in his fifties. If he'd been forced to continue playing the same music he played with Bernstein at 8, he would not have become a world-renowned master. Everyone can recognize that fact and agree with it. So why do managers and organizations ignore it when it involves their employees? What is the difference between holding back the development of an 8-year-old Yo-Yo Ma and holding back the development of a 20-something or 30-something individual working in a commercial or governmental organization? How many employees in your company have never been given the chance to develop their potential? Perhaps you will find it best to plead the Fifth Amendment with regard to that question, on the grounds that the answer may be self-incriminating.

Charles O'Reilly and Jeff Pfeffer hit the nail on the head in their book *Hidden Value*:

The unfortunate mathematical fact is that only 10 percent of the people are going to be in the top 10 percent. So, companies have a choice. They can all chase the same supposed talent. Or they can ... build an organization that helps make it possible for regular folks to perform as if they were in the top 10 percent.

Do you think there are lots of 'regular' people – i.e. not the currently acknowledged stars – in your organization who are capable of performing like the top 10 percent? We do. We've worked with tens of thousands of people in Europe, North America, Asia and Australia over the last 40 years, helping them and their companies recognize their abilities and their capabilities.

Because organizations work on the assumption that 'you know talent when you see it', they 'see' what they want to see, they chase the alleged 10 percent, and they miss a vast array of talented people. Yo-Yo Ma was easy to spot because very few 4-year-olds can play a cello, but nobody spotted Rolf Harris as a highly talented painter. If anything, based on his early performance, they would have earmarked him as an Olympic athlete: at 16 he was the Australian Junior 110 metre backstroke champion. He only began painting seriously much later in life.

Did anyone recognize the talent of H. David Sanders when they saw it? He was a rather unsuccessful insurance salesman, fireman and steamboat captain. But he went on to found a multi-billion-dollar business with a presence around the globe. We know him as Colonel Sanders, of Kentucky Fried Chicken fame.

Talent is situation specific

Did the board of Home Depot know talent, in the person of Bob Nardelli at GE, when they saw it? They thought so and they made him CEO. There is no doubt that he was, and is, a highly talented executive. However, six years later, with the Home Depot stock price still lower than when he joined the company, they fired him. Talent is not general, it's situation specific. We wouldn't expect Yo-Yo Ma to become a talented finance director because the role is far removed from that of a virtuoso cellist. But we might guess that a talented number two executive like Nardelli, from a giant corporation like GE, would become a talented chief executive at a different company. But *how* different? Is being a successful CEO transferable across any organization? The answer, as many successful-in-one-company and unsuccessful-in-another CEOs will attest, is No.

General talent transfer approaches don't typically work

Some years ago we worked on a longitudinal study of about 400 Xerox managers across Europe to identify talent. The specific question the company asked was: 'Who has the talent to be promoted?' The international HR manager at the time arranged to have the managers complete a battery of diagnostic questionnaires under controlled conditions. These included IQ, personality, skill and behaviour measures. When the data had been collected and he looked at the results, he wasn't able to draw any conclusions. The data were then given to us to see if we could find any useful information. On the basis that the skills, ability, preferences and behaviour that lead to high-level performance are situational, we carefully segmented the individuals by function, job type and organizational level and, by conducting a gap analysis between their current profile and the profile required for the next step up, were able to identify with 85 percent accuracy who would be successful at a next-level job.

However, what we discovered was that talent in one functional area of the company was not generally transferable to another functional area. People who were talented finance managers were not successful in marketing, etc. Nor were talented managers in one country unit necessarily able to perform at the same level of competence in a different culture.

Recognizing potential

There is more to talent than simply being able to deliver superior performance in the present. There are two sides to the issue of who your best people are: first the level of their *a*bility (current performance); second, the level of their *cap*ability (potential performance). Identifying, attracting, developing and retaining talented people requires a focus on both of these things. Too often companies fall into the experience trap – seeking and hiring people on the basis that they have done something before, rather than focusing on what they are capable of doing in the future. But biography is not destiny; you aren't trapped by your past and you *can* do different things in the future.

Organizations resemble living organisms in many ways. Unless they grow and change they die. The ability to adapt allows them to live for very long periods of time but failure to adjust to societal changes sounds a death knell. Being able to change and adapt means that you have to have people with the full opportunity to utilize their potential. That's really what talent management is about – creating structures and processes that enable people to discover and exploit their capabilities to the greatest personal and organizational benefit, and getting managers to implement and support these structures and processes.

Adaptability and potential

One of the outstanding characteristics of human beings is their ability to adjust to changing circumstances. It's what has allowed the species to survive and become dominant. But some people are less flexible than others. We must accept that.

However, by and large people have a much wider range of capability than we, and they, believe. By just looking at what people can do currently and projecting that on to what they can supposedly do in the future, organizations fail to capitalize on the huge reservoir of potential that exists in everyone.

The concept of Best people: a better way of approaching the talent question

Try to forget about the word talent for a moment. It smacks of leaping buildings in a single bound, moving faster than a speeding bullet and being more powerful than a locomotive, all of which, as you will recall, are the phrases used to describe Superman. Talent is a word that is hard to escape because it has found its way into the current management jargon. We will use it in various places throughout this book, but please bear in mind that when we do, we mean *the ability and the capability to do something well.* But we'd like to take it one further step and tie the word 'well' down with some form of measurement. In fact we want to change the word 'well' to 'best'. We want to move from talking about who your talented people are (who have the ability and capacity to do something well), to who your *best* people are, because 'best' is much easier to understand.

Defining 'Best'

Performance is job specific. If we say someone is a good performer, what we mean is that he or she is performing well in their current job. The performance is the result of behaviour in the present – not just any behaviour, but the *right* behaviour for the job or task. A simple example is selling. If a group of individuals each have the task to sell X amount of product or service over Y amount of time, and some consistently meet the target while others don't, it is the *behaviour* of the successful ones that makes the difference. The specific sales task in question requires that the salesperson does certain things (behaviours). If he or she does

> " 'Best' occurs when the individual's behaviour matches the behaviour demands of the job "

those things, success occurs; if they don't, failure occurs. In order to be performed most effectively, every job requires its incumbent to apply a certain set of behaviours. *'Best' occurs when the individual's behaviour matches the behaviour demands of the job.*

Defining 'Best' – behaviour specifications

Who are your Best people? They are the people who demonstrate the ability and capability to do what their job requires excellently. They make the highest sales, they satisfy all their customers, they deliver what they promise, they meet all their deadlines, they work well in their teams, they generate the greatest enthusiasm, and they consistently achieve their objectives. *They do precisely what the job requires.* And jobs change constantly. While change was exceptional 50 years ago, it's a given today. Job descriptions (role specifications) are out of date almost as soon as they are produced. What's needed are *behaviour* specifications – a precise list of the specific behaviours that are necessary to produce high-level performance in a job – and they need to be updated constantly.

The results of matching behaviour to the situation – creating Best behaviour

When managers match their behaviour to meet the demands of the role and situation – i.e. are Best – they produce significant results. We've worked with a global Fortune 200 company over the past few years to help them develop behaviour specifications for their top 350 or so senior managers and the work has paid off in significantly increased performance. The company set a target to double revenues over a period of five years. We began work with the senior executive group of 67 people at the back end of 2003 so that the first set of behaviour specifications were in place at the start of 2004. Using a behaviour diagnostic, the MCPI Performance

Improvement Profile (an organizational diagnostic that identifies and measures 400 specific behaviours), we produced precise current behaviour blueprints for each of the 67 executives in the senior team – i.e. what each of them were doing currently to generate performance – plus what each of them thought they needed to be doing to improve performance (for those who may be interested, the details of the diagnostic are provided in the Appendix). We aggregated the data and presented it to them in Q1 of 2004. The following chart is a summary of the data for the senior executive group at the end of 2003.

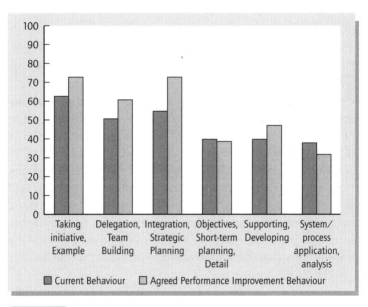

figure 1.1 Behaviour profile end 2003

Present versus future behaviours – the improvement target

In the chart, the dark shaded bars show the benchmark behaviour of the senior executive group at the end of 2003. The lightly shaded bars show the behaviour which the senior executives agreed would enable them to improve their performance – their behaviour specifications – i.e. the behaviour which they agreed would best meet the demands of the situation in 2004.

Each individual's MCPI Performance Improvement Profile (PIP) output generates (1) a list of the top 20 specific behaviours with which they drive their current performance and (2) a list of the 20 behaviours they believe would improve their performance. While there is generally some overlap between these two lists, the latter reveals a number of things that individuals can do to perform better, but on which they are currently not focusing time and energy. We all know, at the back of our minds, that there are things we can and should do differently, but the constant daily pressures of work tend to prevent us from stepping back and taking the time to think the issues through. The Performance Improvement Profile enables people to articulate these ideas.

Because the situation has such a powerful influence over people's behaviour, one tends to find that the individuals who comprise groups, like the senior team of the company in question, have similar thoughts about what they need to do to improve performance. They may each approach the situation from different points of view, functions, sub-markets and sub-cultures, but often there is a set of key behaviours which they all believe need to be emphasized, but to which none of them is currently giving attention. This was the case here. The Performance Improvement Profile (PIP) showed that 57 of the 67 managers (i.e. 85 percent of them) believed that in order to increase revenues they needed to focus energy and attention on the following six behaviours – but none of them was currently doing so:

- Align goals and objectives across team.
- Encourage people to take considered risks.
- Focus on the integration of activities and results.
- Make actions clear and transparent to all.
- Focus performance improvement on areas with major future impact.
- Ask people what they need to do to make a difference.

A musical comedy written by Cole Porter had a hit song which declared that Fifty million Frenchmen can't be wrong. The same argument applies here. If four or five people in a group of 67 think something should be done, it's perhaps a topic for discussion. If 85 percent of them think the same, it has to be right.

The next chart shows the degree to which what the group said they would do compared to what they actually did.

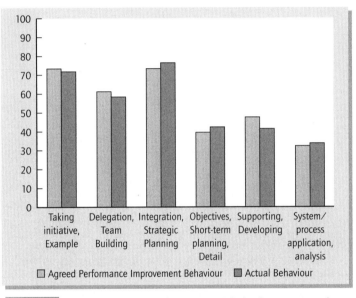

figure 1.2 Agreed performance improvement behaviour vs. Actual behaviour 2004

Closing the opportunity gap

The lightly shaded bars represent the behaviours on which the senior executive groups agreed they should focus during 2004 to drive their performance, and the dark shaded bars show what they actually did. They stuck to what the analysis showed they should do, and as a result revenues increased by 10 percent.

At the start of 2005 they went through the process again. The situation at the beginning of 2005 was different from that of a year before. For one thing they now had a clear strategic plan in place and had adopted a more active and direct leadership role. This time the agreed performance improvement focus was placed on behaviours linked to delegating and driving responsibility down the organization, and on execution (closely tracking performance against short-term objectives and plans). The next chart shows the 2005 agreed performance improvement behaviour and what they actually did.

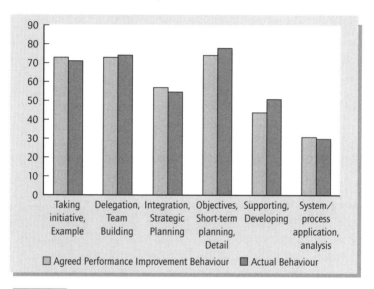

figure 1.3 Agreed performance improvement behaviour vs. Actual behaviour 2005

Once again we analyzed their Performance Profile data and found four behaviours which they all agreed required priority focus, but were not currently being given adequate attention. The behaviours this time were:

- Let people make necessary changes to get things done.
- Assess performance on an on-going basis.
- Get people to commit publicly to performance schedules and time frames.
- Set a standard of performance excellence.

It perhaps needs to be made clear that these behaviours were not being completely ignored. They just weren't being emphasized. Research indicates that 80 percent of performance tends to be driven by about 20 specific behaviours. We all do hundreds of different things, but some of them have a much greater effect than others. It's important to know what these things are.

As a result, once again, of focusing on what the analysis showed they should do, revenues increased by 28 percent in 2005.

We won't bore you with more data and graphs, but they repeated the process again at the start of 2006 and revenues increased by 34 percent. They were up again in 2007 and the company is well within reach of their target of doubling revenues by 2009. Changing behaviour to meet the demands of the situation generates results.

You can manage what you can measure

There is no question that managing talent effectively is important. More than 90 percent of managers agree. They just don't know how to get their hands around the problem and part of the reason is the lack of agreement about what talent is, and even more to the point, how to measure it. However, if we move from the rather amorphous concept of talent to the sharp definition of *Best* – the match between an individual's behaviour and the behaviour demands of the job – the problem is more easily resolved.

Criteria and calibration

If we think of how gymnastics judges decide on their assessments of athletes' performance and we apply the same principles to measuring Best in terms of how well people are operating in their jobs, the issue of identifying who your Best people are becomes simpler. The essence of the system is that gymnastics judges *have a clear set of criteria against which to calibrate performance*. Without clear and objective criteria, the whole thing falls down. And, rather importantly, these criteria are *behaviours*. As we said earlier, in gymnastics you get points if you do some things, and lose points if you don't do some things. The reason there are a number of judges (apart from political issues at international events) is that the movements of the contestants – their behaviours – are rapid and not easy to follow precisely. More eyes see more details. If the events were videotaped and played back in slow motion, one judge would be sufficient.

Precisely the same thing applies to measuring performance in a job. In order for the job to be done best, its incumbent has to *do* certain things – e.g. set clear objectives, or plan carefully, or set out challenges, or give detailed instructions, or provide help and support, or delegate responsibility, or set an example, etc. For every job there are a number of essential things that must be done (behaviours) in order to achieve its objectives.

Measuring the 'how'

We all know there is no single list of criteria (behaviours) that universally describes Best in terms of every job or every person. Jobs are all different from one another and the things that must be done to perform them most effectively are different. What we are talking about is *job behaviour specification*. Most organizations have developed role specifications – the *what* of the job – but almost none have behaviour specifications – the *how* of the job.

To achieve a 10-out-of-10 you need to know what a 10 looks like

Performance is the result of behaviour. It's what you *do* that makes the difference, not what you think, feel, hope, fear, want or wish. And if you do the right things at the right time, you get optimal performance. There is a specific set of key behaviours for every job that produces high-level performance. These are the criteria against which Best is measured. If the job holder does everything required by the job – i.e. demonstrates all the correct behaviours in the appropriate proportion –

> " it's what you *do* that makes the difference, not what you think, feel, hope, fear, want or wish "

they *must* get a rating of Best. They can't do better. If someone says 'You could have done better', that implies that they should have done some different things – i.e. behaved differently. But if they have done everything the job requires in terms of behaviour, then they *can't* do better; a change in behaviour can only be counter-productive.

When Tiger Woods hits a four iron from well out in the fairway and it rolls into the hole, that's a perfect 10. The required behaviour for the task is a four iron hit with precisely that power and in that precise direction. Golfers constantly ask the question 'What shot do I need to play here?' Tennis players ask themselves the same thing, only much more rapidly. Why don't managers ask themselves the question 'What should I do now?' as they manage their jobs, and understand that it means 'What *behaviour* should I use now?'

What we will show you in this book is how to do that. And we will also show you how you can give everyone in the organization that information, and get a very clear assessment of their ability and their potential. And once you've done that, you can help them reach their potential without huge fuss and vast expense. You can help them be the best they can be, and in doing so make the organization the best it can be.

Who wants to be Best?

The harsh reality, unfortunately, is that not everyone wants to be the best they can be, but we believe this is often because they don't know how. Nor have they been given the opportunity and the support to help make it happen. Winston Churchill remarked that 'Success is going from failure to failure without loss of enthusiasm', but it takes a very strong self-concept to brush failure aside. Companies babble on about helping their people to learn from failure and they put a caring and supportive spin on it. But more often than not, the 'learning' is painful. What the person learns is never to do anything differently again, never to take initiative and never to take risk. We've seen hundreds of managers who have been written off by their companies because of a single failure, and often a rather unimportant one. The most difficult part of getting people to rise to their best is to get them to believe they *can*. The great tennis star Venus Williams says, 'You have to believe in yourself when no one else does', but for all but the strongest of people that's not always easy. Good talent management helps people build self-belief.

Motivation to achieve

Wanting to do something and doing it are two different things. Vince Lombardi commented that, 'The only place success comes before work is in the dictionary.' To be Best requires work and the willingness to work. We don't labour under the delusion that everyone is motivated to improve their performance or that everyone will take the opportunity to reach their potential. There are lots of people with so-called natural talent who have never risen to any real level of success. People who are not interested in becoming the best they can be aren't necessarily lacking skill or ability; they simply lack the will. We know that applies to many people in the workplace. But we also know that they are in the minority and that most people, if given the opportunity to expand their abilities and to explore their capabilities, will grasp the chance.

The 'Best' acid test

To find out who wants to be a Best person, look at how they deal with opportunity. If you allow self-nomination for training and development, who puts themselves forward? If you offer people more responsibility (and accountability), who takes it? If you publicize openings for jobs, who applies? If you lay down challenges for people, who responds? Sometimes if you ask people if they're willing to do something they will say yes, but saying they will is not the same as actually doing it. *The acid test is observable behaviour.*

> to find out who wants to be a Best person, look at how they deal with opportunity

Aubrey Daniels, author of *Bringing Out the Best in People*, one of the very best books on motivating people, says, 'Every organizational accomplishment is dependent on behaviour. Whenever an organization strives to improve quality, increase productivity, or

boost creativity, it must ask people to change their behaviour.'
And, he says, it is a myth that people resist change; 'The reality is
that change is natural and almost always accepted when it produces something positive for the performer.'

Chapter summary

▦ Talent is everywhere. You just have to know how to look for it
and how to manage it.

▦ Research indicates that formalizing talent management is good
for business – higher earnings, higher net margins, higher ROA
and ROE, and greater competitive edge.

▦ Talent is defined as 'the ability and the capability to do something
well'. It's not just about the present (ability), it's also about the
future (capability). The latter is the key to effective talent
development – recognizing and releasing people's potential.

▦ Ability and capability are not about traits, personality or genes
– they're about *behaviour*. Unlike genetics or personality,
behaviour can be described, observed, measured and changed.
As a result, both ability and capability can be increased.

▦ Rather than talk about talent, which is a word loaded with a
number of connotations, we use the term 'Best'.

*'Best' occurs when the individual's behaviour matches the
behaviour demands of the job.*

▦ The answer to the question 'Who are your Best people?' is
straightforward. It is those people who do precisely what is
required to perform their jobs excellently. Because this is about
behaviour that is observable and measurable, the assessment of
Best is rational and objective.

▦ Job *role* specifications outline the **what** (goals, targets,
objectives). To create Best performance, an additional element
is required – a job *behaviour* specification (the **how**).

Questions to ask yourself

- As a manager, what could you do to identify and develop the talent in your organization?
  - Do you actively encourage suggestions and new ways of doing things?
  - Do you give people opportunity to talk about how best to use their strengths?
  - Do you listen and act upon their inputs?
  - Are you currently building your own succession plan?
- Do you know who your Best people are?
  - What is it that they are doing that makes them stand out?
  - Do you know how they do what they do?
  - Can you describe this in specific behaviours?
- Do you know who your Best people could be?
  - What are you doing to encourage and harness this talent?
  - What is the single thing that each person could do to help achieve their potential?
- Do all your people know what they need to do to be most effective – to be Best – in their current roles?
  - Have you specified the behaviours that are important to each role?
  - Does your organization currently have a robust way of helping you to do this easily?

From a different angle

An American colleague of ours, Bill Kuhn, has wide experience with the management of talent. He has run, worked for, and consulted to a number of America's best-performing and best-managed companies and he has written a brief article for us at the end of each of the next chapters, which we have titled 'From a Different Angle'. Bill talks about the practical application of the concepts discussed in each chapter and gives examples of how talent can be managed most effectively. You will find his pieces interesting, provocative and helpful.

2

How can you identify Best people?

As I grow older I pay less attention to what men say. I just watch what they do.

Andrew Carnegie

Only a mediocre person is always at his best.

Lawrence Peter

Almost everyone has some talent. The question is: talent for what? Individuals can be good at any number of things – flying an aeroplane, fishing, stealing cars, teaching children, playing football, selling, designing machines, leading people, etc. What we're interested in here is talent in terms of the ability to do things that help an organization perform well. Every organization has performance objectives and therefore every organization needs to have people with the ability and capacity to do things that enable them to achieve these objectives.

The real measure of a Best performer is not how well they perform at one task or at one time, but how they perform over a period of time. This implies the ability to adapt one's behaviour to different situations, different competition and different behavioural demands.

Michael Johnson is recognized as one of the best athletes of all time, not simply because at the 1996 Olympics he won the gold medal and set a world record for the 400 metres, but also because he won gold for the 200 metres, the only male athlete ever to win both events at the same Olympics. On top of that, he holds world records in the 200 metre, 400 metre and 4×400 metre relay, and 300 metres. Plus he won a gold medal in the 1992 Olympics and two in 2000 and won nine World Championship gold medals between 1991 and 1999. That's not a flash in the pan, that's Best.

Jack Welch's career at GE can be rated as Best because over the 20 years he led the company, its market capitalization increased by more than $400 billion. We can say that as an author of fantasy literature, J.K. Rowling is Best because she hasn't written one best-selling book, she's written a series of them that have sold more than 400 million copies. She's the first person ever to become a dollar billionaire from book royalties.

Talent is all around us

There is far more talent around than we believe, and it manifests itself in an infinite number of ways. For instance, there are 1,140,000 entries on Google for 'Halls of Fame'. There are more than one thousand halls of fame in the US alone and each of the individuals who are honoured in them is there because of their exceptional performance in a particular field of endeavour. Talent has millions of different faces, and if you want an idea of the variety, here are a few halls of fame you might not have heard about:

" talent has millions of different faces "

- The Australian Stockman's Hall of Fame
- The Mad Scientist Network Hall of Fame
- The Hall of Fame of Them (aliens in the desert)
- The Bead Researchers Hall of Fame
- The Kiwi Bingo Winners Hall of Fame
- The Pirate Radio Hall of Fame
- The Mariachi Hall of Fame

The criteria for admission to various halls of fame vary widely. Talent is defined in any number of ways. Interestingly, the International Institute of Management does not include Jack Welch on either its list of the World's Most Respected CEOs or its list of the 50 Most Influential Management Thinkers, but Scott Adams (the creator of the Dilbert cartoon character) makes the list, as does Martha Stewart, a convicted felon.

Identifying talent is currently a bit of a hit-and-miss affair. For instance, management recruiters tend to focus on the low-hanging fruit – graduates from the top universities – and compete fiercely for them. The average salary for MBA graduates from Harvard, Stanford, INSEAD and the London Business School in 2005 was about $125,000 plus signing bonuses of $25,000 to $30,000. However, while recruiters paid higher salaries to graduates of top-tier business schools, a study done at Pace University in 2006 showed that the performance of CEOs from prestigious universities was no different from the performance of those who had graduated from less prestigious schools.

What's the starting point to identify 'Best'?

While identifying talented people and then finding jobs where they can exercise their talent creates a danger of excluding people who have potential but haven't been sprinkled with talent stardust, going to the other extreme of identifying jobs and then looking for talented people to fill them also has pitfalls. There is a basic flaw in the logic of both approaches, which centres on the underlying assumption both make that 'you will recognize talent when you see it'. Since we know you won't, what should you do?

The 'Right Stuff' myth

When trying to look for talent, what's the starting point? Should we try to identify the traits, characteristics, attitudes, motivations and behaviours of talented people – people who continually succeed at a variety of things? The business world's view of talent is somewhat Darwinian: the belief is that those with innate talent survive challenge after challenge and rise to the top, whereas those that don't have 'the Right Stuff' fall somewhere along the way. It will come as no surprise that the main champions of this view are people who have succeeded in rising to the top of organizations and who (conveniently forgetting any of their little stumbles along the way) are keen on awarding themselves superhero status. We call this *the Invincibility Syndrome*.

The Invincibility Syndrome

The Invincibility Syndrome is quite easy to create. Armies have used the technique many times. When there is a mission for which nobody in their right minds would knowingly volunteer, they ask for volunteers for a 'challenging, demanding, and very important task'. (You have to make it sound attractive because the target is to get a large number of volunteers, say 1,000.) The volunteers are then put through a series of exercises/tests and after each test, 50 percent are failed. After the tenth task there will be only one person left and anyone who has seen 999 keen and capable people fail while he or she has emerged victorious in not just one difficult and challenging situation, but *ten* of them in a row, is highly likely to believe that they are significantly more capable than their peers.

Put that into an organizational context. Someone who has been promoted over his or her peers 10 or 15 times, with accompanying increased sycophancy at each promotion, can be forgiven for thinking themselves as, if not invincible, then at least infallible. Add a reward structure that pays the individual vast amounts of money and it is the rare person who can, to paraphrase the saying, 'keep their head while all around them are losing theirs'. If you were one of these individuals, wouldn't you believe that talented people are born not made, and that the blue blood of True Talent ran strongly in your veins? It's one of the reasons why the myth of 'having the Right Stuff' persists.

In his book *High Flyers*, Morgan McCall makes the interesting observation that 'Executive leaders demonstrate that they have the right stuff by amassing a track record of performance under difficult circumstances (but that is only) determined *after* remarkable performance has been achieved.' If talent can only be defined in terms of having survived challenge after challenge, then there are a couple of problems. The first problem is that we can't be sure who has talent until a lot of water has gone under the bridge. And the second problem is that the definition of talent is an exercise in circular logic. As McCall puts it, 'The right stuff is whatever it needs to be to explain a result.'

Always start with the job and define Best behaviours

The start point for identifying Best is the job. Think of the earlier example of gymnastics. The perfect score of 10 is derived from the *behaviour specifications* of the routine. Demonstrate all the behaviours perfectly and the routine must be awarded a perfect 10 – i.e. 'Best'. The criteria are based not on the 'talent' of the competitor – i.e. if he or she 'could do' moves x, y and z, or may have done them in the past – but on the actual demonstration of the required moves at the critical time. That's the athlete's 'job'. The difference between it and many jobs in organizations is that the latter almost never have clearly stated behaviour specifications. Make no mistake: *there is a specific set of behaviours that will produce optimal performance in every job.* All that's needed is a mechanism that will enable organizations to identify that set of behaviours.

This approach works for determining capability (future performance) as well as ability (current performance). Once again it hinges on the ability to define the set of specific behaviours that are necessary to produce optimal performance in a new or different job. Once these are known, one can do two things: (1) ask the individual whether he or she is able to do these things, and (2) test to see if the individual can do them. 'Can you jump six feet?', 'Yes', 'OK, let me see you do it'. 'Can you get people involved and enthusiastic?', 'Yes', 'OK, show me how you do it.'

Best is about *behaviour*. It is about doing the things that the job requires, and not doing the things that it doesn't require – i.e. not doing things that waste time and energy or get in the way of achieving the key objectives. Potential Best is also about behaviour. It's about giving an individual the opportunity to see if he or she can do what the job requires and to provide support in the learning process. Best people don't pop out of a shell fully formed like the goddess Aphrodite. First they need to know how Best is defined – i.e. what specific behaviours they need to be able to demonstrate – and then they need to work on how to demonstrate them effectively. But there is no simple set of Best behaviours, no one size fits all. Best behaviour varies with the job and few jobs are exactly the same.

> **Best behaviour varies with the job and few jobs are exactly the same**

Examples of Best behaviour for six different jobs

To illustrate this, here are examples of six quite different jobs and the behaviours necessary to perform them most effectively. The data are from the analytic output of the *Momentum CPI Performance Improvement Profile* (PIP) behavioural diagnostic (Appendix A).

The six roles we have chosen to illustrate the differences in required behaviour across different jobs are:

- Finance Manager
- HR Manager
- Information Systems Manager
- Operations Improvement Manager
- Sales Manager
- Maintenance Manager

Please note that these are *not* generic roles. They are the jobs of six *particular* managers in six different companies. There is no generic set of behaviours for Finance, HR, IT, Ops, Sales and Maintenance managers. Effective behaviour is situational. Managers may have similar job titles but it is the requirements and context of their jobs – company, structure, culture, etc. – that determines what they need to do to perform well.

An initial differentiating measure between these particular jobs is the balance of performance-accelerating and performance-sustaining behaviour which each of them requires.

▓ **Accelerating behaviours** Performance-accelerating behaviours are actions that move things forward, change the way things are done, and improve overall effectiveness. They are centred on vision, change and improving effectiveness.

▓ **Sustaining behaviours** Performance-sustaining behaviours are actions that are aimed at making things run smoothly, that ensure plans are implemented, targets achieved and quality is maintained. They are centred on implementation, consistency, attention to detail and improving efficiency.

	Finance Manager	HR Manager	Information Systems Manager	Operations Improvement Manager	Sales Manager	Maintenance Manager
Performance accelerating/ sustaining focus	Accelerating	Sustaining	Equal emphasis accelerating/ sustaining	Accelerating	Sustaining	Equal emphasis accelerating/ sustaining

But while is it useful to know the degree to which one should focus on performance-accelerating or performance-sustaining behaviour, what is critical is to know the *specific* behaviours that will drive performance.

The 80:20 performance law

Research indicates that about 15–20 of the things (behaviours) that managers do account for about 80 percent of their performance. What we want to illustrate is that there are significantly different behavioural demands for different jobs, and that there is a relative handful of specific things that determine performance in each job. We won't burden you with long lists of the behaviours required for effective performance in each of our sample jobs. Let's only look at the top (most important) five behaviours that the incumbents of each of our six different jobs recognize as being most critical to achieving Best performance. More complete behaviour specifications for these jobs would list the key 15 to 20 behaviours, but the following will suffice to illustrate our point.

The Finance Manager's job

- Assess the future implications of decisions.
- Get people to focus on how they can make their best contribution.
- Generate enthusiasm and excitement.
- Create integrative processes and systems.
- Cultivate a range of contacts throughout the company.

The HR Manager's job

- Get people to identify and implement best practice.
- Require people to commit formally to plans and objectives.
- Require proposals to have factual data to support them.
- Review and clarify people's objectives with them.
- Seek out ideas and suggestions from people.

The Information Systems Manager's job

- Help people develop the necessary skills for their jobs.
- Always meet commitments.
- Face up to and deal with demanding situations.
- Allow individuals scope to change how they manage their jobs.
- Back up the team's ideas and initiatives for change.

The Operations Improvement Manager's job

- Get people committed to common objectives.
- Encourage people to take considered risks.
- Create a shared commitment to what has to be done.
- Create a sense of urgency.
- Constantly suggest ideas to increase effectiveness.

The Sales Manager's job

■ Separate broad policy goals into manageable objectives.

■ Transfer as much responsibility to people as they can manage.

■ Always meet commitments.

■ Encourage contributions from everyone.

■ Give people opportunities to display their ability.

The Maintenance Manager's job

■ Help people develop the necessary skills for their jobs.

■ Get people committed to common objectives.

■ Constantly suggest ideas to increase effectiveness.

■ Give people frequent performance feedback.

■ Back up the team's ideas and initiatives for change.

As you look at these lists of behaviours, you'll notice there is very little duplication. The six jobs in question are quite different from one another and therefore it should not come as a surprise that the behaviour required to perform them effectively will be different.

" Best occurs when the individual's behaviour matches the behaviour demands of the job "

Best occurs when the individual's behaviour matches the behaviour demands of the job. Therefore Best can only be defined in terms of the job.

Calibrating performance

How do you identify Best people? You start by creating behaviour specifications for each job and then you match the individual's current behaviour with that specification. The effectiveness with which an individual manages his or her job – i.e. the level of performance that is achieved (Best) – is dependent on the degree to which their behaviour matches the behavioural demands of the job. If the individual is doing 80 percent of the things the job requires, he or she is 80 percent of the way to being Best; if 60 percent, then 60 percent of the way to being Best, etc. The diagram below illustrates this. The greater the overlap of the two circles, the closer to achieving Best performance.

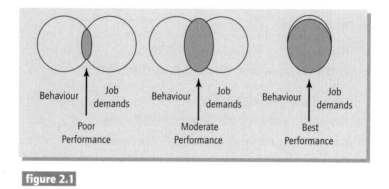

figure 2.1

Chapter summary

- The real measure of an individual's talent (ability and capability) is not how well they perform at one task or at one time, but how they perform over a period of time.

- The most appropriate way of identifying Best is the job itself. There is a unique and specific set of behaviours which will produce optimal performance in every job. This is the point of creating job-behaviour specifications.

- 15 to 20 behaviours account for roughly 80 percent of a manager's professional performance.

- Best occurs when the individual's behaviour matches the behaviour demands of the job. Therefore *Best can only be defined in terms of the job itself.*

From a different angle

Want to identify and manage talent? Ask Bob

We tend to think it's the major corporations that have the resources and capabilities to perform well and excel in people management. I often find – and studies support this – that smaller companies can do as well, if not better, in areas such as identifying, developing and managing talent, in part because they're not weighed down by intrusive systems, procedures and bureaucracy. Frequently, Generations X and Y are finding that smaller companies are friendlier, express more interest in them as a person, and give them greater opportunity to be rewarded for their talents.

The ability to identify, develop and empower Best people so that they can fully realize their potential and add significant value to the organization is not confined to the heads of big businesses. CEOs of smaller businesses can be equally adept. A case in point is Bob Jaster, the past CEO of The Robinson Brick Company. In 1995, the company recruited Bob as Vice-President of Manufacturing, promoted him to Chief Operations Officer in 1999, and in 2000, the owner (fourth generation in the Robinson family) appointed him President and CEO, the first outsider in the company's 120-year history to ever to assume that position.

Bob ranks as one of the very best CEOs I have ever worked with. Under his leadership, in the seven-year period from 1999 to 2006, the company's revenues rose from $24 million to almost $100 million and profits increased from slightly under $2 million to $12 million. The company expanded into natural stone, made selective acquisitions in the west and mid-western parts of the United States, and became known as the most technologically advanced brick manufacturer in North America. It became the first brick manufacturer in North America to achieve the international quality standard ISO 9001, and in 2003 met the highest standard, ISO 9001-2000. In seven years Bob Jaster turned Robinson Brick into the premier brick manufacturer, sought after by the major world brick players. And he built the company's value from $13 million to $116 million when it was sold in 2006 to the giant Austrian-based firm, Weinberger AG.

How did he do that? Part of the answer is the way he managed and developed the people in the company, identifying potential and then helping them grow their skills and abilities. He began by turning his group of direct reports into an excellent team. There were re-assignments – a few to lesser responsibility when they couldn't meet the challenges Bob set out – but his people stayed with him. Most of his managers were given what Bob referred to as 'stretch' goals, as well as broader responsibilities, some a radical departure from what they had been doing. For example, the head of Human Resources ulti-mately took on the responsibility of marketing and IT, as well as HR.

Bob's philosophy is: Give them responsibility, challenge them, and see what they do with it. Tell them they're the best, and they'll come to believe it and act accordingly. His articulation of this philosophy stands as the beacon of what every manager who aspires to greatness should believe and be doing: 'I want to make every direct report highly marketable, so they can have such a résumé of achievements that they can always move on to an even better job if they choose to leave.' There is no better description of a manager's principal responsibility and no better explanation of why Bob's achievements at Robinson Brick were so outstanding.

Having talent is one thing, but applying it is quite another, and Bob understands that clearly. At board meetings he frequently made the point that while talent is important, the ability to apply that talent (i.e. behaviour) is more important. How employees perform (behaviour) will affect the entire organization. He believes that you don't know true talent until you understand all the behavioural issues, and that 'talent cannot be viewed as a gift; it must be earned'. He asks the following questions: 'Does the person have the passion, is he or she willing to make sacrifices, and take risk? Is the person committed as an individual, and to the management team and the company?' He is a close observer of how staff accept responsibility and handle authority. His view is that the key to effective performance is what one does with authority, specifically, how one uses power when given responsibility.

I asked Bob how he identified 'Best people'. He said the most difficult part is when you first get to see them and haven't had an opportunity to observe their behaviour. Often, he says, it can be harder to identify who *doesn't* have talent. He strongly believes you must build trust and loyalty. Once you build mutual trust, then you get feedback. When loyalty is demonstrated and trust is established, then you can get a good idea of the individual and see true talent. Only with truth can you focus on resources and talent.

Bob Jaster believes that managers must be prepared to accept the risk of their people failing from time to time. He says you have to trust them and allow people to be successful and not 'rob them of success'. I asked if he had ever been burned. 'Oh yes, for some of those who are highly talented, it takes time to know if they will use that talent positively or negatively, and when they are not only talented but extremely bright as well, that's even harder to figure out.' But despite his answer, it doesn't look as though he has been mistaken too many times. If you want to identify and manage talent, ask Bob.

Bill Kuhn

Questions to ask yourself

- When you look at how you discuss job roles and agree objectives, how much time, proportionately, do you spend on the *what* (Key Performance Indicators, targets, objectives) and how much on the *how* (behaviours)?
- When you look at the roles of people in your team and their current performance levels, what do you see as the key improvement areas?
- Who is in a role that requires different behaviours to what he or she is currently doing? What effect is this having on results? What could they do differently to become Best?
- Do you have a clear approach to dealing with these situations?

3

How can you create Best people?

Don't hire great leaders, make your own.

Harvard Business School's Programme for Leadership
Development

Outstanding leaders go out of their way to boost the self-esteem of their personnel. If people believe in themselves, it's amazing what they can accomplish.

Sam Walton

Marcus Buckingham asks the key question about managing talent: 'What would happen if men and women spent more than 75 percent of each day on the job using their strongest skills and engaged on their favourite tasks, basically doing exactly what they wanted to do?' It's a question that runs a shiver down the spines of many managers. A recent cover of *Fortune* that pictured two young 20-something people with the heading 'Manage US? Puh-leeze ...' encapsulated the fears of loss of control that plague traditional managers. But there's nothing new about this. The increase in the level of education of the workforce in the Western world has led to an increased sense of independence.

People don't leave bad companies – they leave bad managers

There's no reason why people have to put up with bad management, lousy leadership and a dull and boring job. But it appears that many organizations haven't caught on. In 2007 the coaching company Ros Taylor asked 1,500 employees what they thought of their bosses: 90 percent said their boss did nothing about poor performance; 89 percent said their boss was unreceptive to new ideas; and 77 percent said their boss was not interested in them. That's hardly what we would call creating Best people!

To get back to Buckingham's question: how would you describe people who spend more than 75 percent of their working day doing what they like doing most? Loose cannons? Undisciplined? Uncontrollable? Or would you take the opposite view and see them as: highly motivated? highly satisfied? highly productive? being personally best? being organizationally best?

Our money is on the second set of descriptors. These people would be like the Seven Dwarfs – whistling on the way to work. But would they meet the definition for 'Best' that we set out in the previous chapter – *'Best' occurs when the individual's behaviour matches the behaviour demands of the job?* Maybe yes and maybe no; it depends on whether their favourite tasks were the tasks that the company wanted done. Doing what you want to do and enjoy doing may be great for you, but it's only great for the organization that pays your salary if it's what *they* need to have done. 'Personal best', to use a sporting term, is not always the same as organizational best.

Focusing and harnessing

But people who spend their time using their strongest skills to do what they love doing tend to produce results. The question is, how can we harness that productivity and focus those results for the organization? The answer is to make sure that people are given jobs that suit both their abilities and capabilities. And the

> 〞 people need to know the *how* as much as they need to know the *what* 〞

second part of the answer is to make sure they understand which behaviours to use to perform the job well. As we noted earlier, people need to know the *how* as much as they need to know the *what*.

Unfortunately that's not what normally happens. Somebody somewhere decides that you should do such-and-such a job. You get asked if you will take the job in a way that tends to leave little doubt that 'no' is not an acceptable answer. So there you are, stuck having to do something you don't particularly want to do, or that you don't feel particularly capable of doing. And to top it all, they don't give you any hints about how to approach the job – what makes it work well. You're just supposed to know.

It's a terrible situation to be in but it's something that occurs in all organizations. But why does it have to be that way? Is it that we think people are intrinsically lazy and that they'll only want to have fun and do as little as possible? Is it that we think that the organization has created a lot of jobs that will simply never be enjoyable or satisfying and therefore if we gave people a choice, none of them would elect to do these jobs? What would be interminably boring to you may be very interesting to me. Why can't we ask people to tell us what they are good at, what they like doing, and most importantly what they think they can do to add most value, and then give them jobs that fulfil those criteria? Does this sound a little idealistic to you? Actually, it's not, it's just that very few managers or organizations have the courage to do it. The Rothmans example that follows shows how it can be done and the huge impact it has on bottom-line performance.

Managing talent effectively

Jeff Pfeffer talks about toxic companies (which he defines as places where people come to work to make enough money to leave) and toxic managers (more about them in Chapter 7). He says that companies that manage people and talent well outperform companies that don't by 30 percent to 40 percent, and this holds true across a wide range of industries from steel to oil, to semi-conductors. People don't have to be managed in a way that devalues, belittles and demotivates them. Pfeffer says that one of the clear signs of a toxic workplace is that the management treat people as if they were what he calls 'a factor of production' – i.e. no different from machines, technology, raw materials, etc. Factors of production are 'things', but people don't like to be thought of and treated like things.

It's what managers do that makes the difference

On the whole, people who like what they are doing tend to perform better than people who don't like what they are doing. But it's not purely a matter of giving people jobs that best suit them, it's doing what Marcus Buckingham's research shows differentiates highly profitable companies from less profitable ones – things like making sure people:

- Know what's expected of them
- Have the resources to do their jobs
- Receive recognition for good work
- Know that their opinions are listened to
- Have opportunities to learn, develop and grow

Pfeffer says, 'You hear a lot about the shortage of talent. The thing to remember is that, for great workplaces, there is no shortage of talent.'

Asking people can make a difference

One of the companies we did a lot of work with some years ago was Rothmans. The CEO was a man called Bill Ryan. He is a very modest and unassuming man but can see things with amazing clarity. And he saw that the way organizations put people into jobs is basically flawed. So he set about doing it differently – to create Best in Rothmans.

One of the things Ryan recognized was the two-sided nature of talent – ability (current performance) and capability (potential performance). And he recognized that a way to unlock the latter was to get people into jobs that, as Marcus Buckingham says, enabled them to spend 'more than 75 percent of each day on the job using their strongest skills'. So he laid out the challenge to the top 300 or so managers in Rothmans around the world: 'Rather than have us tell you what and where your job should be, would you please tell us where you think you would add most value to the company. List the three jobs you think you would be best at and we will do our best to put you in one of them.'

Some of the resultant job shifts were dramatic. One senior line manager who had been in charge of a large business unit in Africa elected to move to a public affairs role in Brussels. Some individuals moved from senior headquarters roles to running national business units. Others moved across divisions, across functions and between country units. And a number elected to stay in their current jobs. The net result was a management which came close to spending more than 75 percent of each day on the job using their strongest skills, basically doing what they wanted to do. And the added bonus was that the company had agreed career plans for everyone. Performance, in terms of revenue and profitability, soared, resulting in a tripling of the value of the company.

Creating Best people

'Best' occurs when the individual's behaviour matches the behaviour demands of the job. Therefore Best people are created by establishing that match. But it's not always easy to do. The behavioural demands of a job are seldom clearly defined. Job descriptions tend to be general in nature and talk more about the *what* than the *how*. Behaviour specifications nail down the *how*, and they do it in a way that can be observed and measured.

Best is not just about onward and upward

Organizations that want to create Best people also need to understand that Best does not have to mean mobility, job change or career progression. Often people are at their best where they are, and moving them or promoting them in order to reward their excellent performance is a formula for failure. Well-known examples include promoting the best sales person to sales manager, the best engineer to manager, a strong functional specialist to general management, etc. Not to say that excellent sales people can't become excellent sales managers, or that engineers or functional specialists can't become excellent senior managers. Of course they can. But not all of them can, and not all of them want to. The only person who can make the decision to move is the person in the job. But that decision cannot be made without certain information. If it wants to create Best people, the organization needs to aid the process by providing help and information and there are a number of key elements it needs to address.

Creating a job behaviour specification for everyone

The first step in creating Best people is to provide them with job behaviour specifications – a blueprint of the specific behaviours that are necessary to perform the job effectively. There are various ways to do this. Competency descriptions can be a starting point for discussions of necessary specific behaviours. They often also add the dimensions of necessary skills and knowledge, both important elements in creating Best.

We tend to cut straight to the chase by asking individuals and their bosses to complete relatively quick and easy MCPI Performance Improvement Profile on-line diagnostic questionnaires. They produce two things: (1) a list of the specific behaviours that the boss believes are critical for top-level performance in the job, and (2) lists of behaviours that the individual is (a) currently giving priority to and (b) believes *should be* given priority. These two outputs are combined in a report that looks like the following:

> This report presents a comparative profile, from the viewpoint of the job holder and his/her manager, of the behaviours required for the job of Integration Manager. Erik Groening is the job holder and Simon Peters is the manager.

Page 1: current behaviours

Among the set of behaviours considered by Simon Peters (the manager) to be important to ensure effective performance in the job of Integration Manager, the following are current high-priority behaviours of Erik Groening (the jobholder) – i.e. these are behaviours to which Erik is currently giving principal emphasis and focus.

- Always meet commitments.
- Constantly suggest ideas to increase effectiveness.
- Face up to and deal with demanding situations.
- Analyze suggested changes thoroughly before taking action.
- Encourage people to find ways to be more effective.
- Transfer as much responsibility to people as they can manage.
- Always try to see the bigger, strategic picture.

Page 2: improvement behaviours

Among the set of behaviours considered by Simon Peters to be important to ensure effective performance in the job of Integration Manager, the following are behaviours that Erik Groening believes have the potential to improve his performance in the job, but to which he is not giving priority:

- Generate enthusiasm and excitement.
- Encourage contributions from everyone.
- Assess the future implications of decisions.
- Give people frequent performance feedback.
- Hold people accountable for their commitments.
- Keep focused on the big issues facing the business.
- Keep on the lookout for dangers and opportunities for the business.

▨ Make it clear to people how their performance is assessed.

▨ Make sure that procedures are helpful rather than obstructive.

▨ Provide clear direction for people.

▨ Provide people with processes that help them work more efficiently.

Page 3: potential behaviours

In addition, Simon Peters considers the following behaviours potentially important to ensure effective performance in the job of Integration Manager. These behaviours are neither currently being given priority focus by Erik Groening nor are among the behaviours he currently thinks will improve his performance.

▨ Get people to identify and implement best practice.

▨ Allow individuals scope to change how they manage their jobs.

▨ Consistently track performance against targets.

▨ Get people committed to common objectives.

▨ Require people to commit formally to plans and objectives.

Given a document of this type, with this information, a discussion between the two individuals will generate a clear and agreed job behaviour specification. The process may begin by getting each of the parties to select the 10 behaviours they believe to be most critical to effective performance in the job. They may wish to reduce these lists even further. Job behaviour specifications should not exceed 20 specific behaviours and these should be sorted into groups of first priority (critical), second priority (important) and third priority (providing additional value). Changing behaviour is an incremental process: you can't change everything at once. Start by focusing on doing three or four specific things, and when these behaviours are embedded, move to the next three or four, and so on.

❝ changing behaviour is an incremental process ❞

The order in which the document is structured reinforces agreement rather than disagreement. In essence, the parties are in agreement on the behaviours on the first two pages. First, on a set of things the incumbent is currently doing that the boss thinks are important. Second, on a set of behaviours that both the boss and job incumbent think would improve performance. The third list is behaviours that the boss believes to be important in producing effective performance in the job, but which are not things that the incumbent is currently doing or has thought might improve his or her performance, but after two sessions of agreement, defensiveness of both parties is significantly reduced. They tend to listen to each other and work easily towards producing a list of behaviours to which both are committed.

The other important factor in this process is that the discussion is focused on specific, observable, measurable behaviour rather than on more subjective and often value-laden things like attitude, motivation or personality. Therefore it is not threatening. Rational arguments can be put forward for each behaviour on the lists, and agreement can be reached.

Self-nomination

If you want to create Best people, one of the first things you need to do is find out who wants is to be Best, and the only way to really do that is to ask people. Create a process of self-nomination for jobs and for training and development. The great majority of talent management programmes and systems are based on nomination by some other individual or group. In most cases, the individuals who have been nominated remain unaware of the fact. Lists of high-potential people, fast-track people, budding leaders and 'talent pool' people are created by various processes but they rely on the opinion of others, not all of whom are unbiased. These opinions are often drawn from performance appraisals which can be highly subjective. Everybody is familiar with managers who hold back people because they don't want to lose them. And everybody is familiar with managers who nominate poor performers or 'difficult' people for transfer or promotion just to get rid of them. Nor is it uncommon to see managers who have favourites whom they support and sponsor over people who have greater talent or potential.

Sometimes people who are put on high-potential lists don't want to be there. Sometimes they're quite happy doing what they are doing, and if they're doing it well, what's wrong with that? If you want to find out who is up for change, for career advancement, for challenge and for performance improvement, the best way is to ask them to identify themselves. Once they've done that, they've passed the first test; they've shown interest and some level of commitment.

Transferring responsibility to the individual

Best people like to feel they have some control over what they do. They don't like to be told. Give individuals who have nominated themselves for challenge, development, job moves, etc. the responsibility to decide on their preferred career paths. Strangely enough, a number of people don't like this; they prefer to have their careers mapped out by others. But we believe they are in the minority and that the reason they are reluctant to take control of their careers is that they don't have the tools with which to engage the process. It's difficult to map out the future starting from the present. It's much easier to start from the future and work back to the present. However, the envisioned future can't be too distant because the further away, the more uncertain and unlikely it appears.

Visioning in practice

Here is an exercise that anyone can usefully engage. Think of where you would like to be five years from today (if five years is too distant a horizon for you, make it four years or three years). What you would like to be doing; who you would like to be working with; where you would like to be; what responsibilities you would like to have; what role you would like, etc. Then, in order to achieve these things

think of where you would like to be five years from today

and be where you want to be in five years' time, where do you need to be in four years' time? And to get there in four years' time, where do you need to be in three years, two years and one year from now? You can't get to the summit unless you are able to get to base camp four, and you can't get to base camp four unless you can make it to base camp three, etc. Having a vision of where you want to end up makes establishing the steps required to get there a lot easier.

Understanding strengths and preferences

Marcus Buckingham talks about the 'strengths revolution' and argues that focusing on strengths rather than weaknesses creates the link to efficiency, competency and success. He says that good managers try to find out what a person's strengths are and to understand what triggers these strengths. He claims that only about 20 percent of people think they are in a job that allows them to do what they do best.

Performance is the result of behaviour (what people *do*) rather than personality (what people *are*). The research is crystal clear on this subject. Personality predicts less than 10 percent of behaviour. However, it does have an important part to play in enabling Best performance. Personality, as a concept, is confused and confusing. There are hundreds of definitions of personality and hundreds of accompanying theories and tests. But the essence of personality is that it is about *preference*. Given the choice, we *prefer* to do certain things and we find certain things more enjoyable than others. If we think in terms of preference, the relationship between personality and Best behaviour becomes clear. Our preferences define a range of behaviours with which we feel comfortable. If we are placed in roles outside this range – i.e. where the required behaviour is not within our preferences – while we can deliver the behaviour in the short term, over the longer term we tend to find it increasingly difficult. We don't like doing these things and therefore we do them increasingly poorly. Lawrence Peter (*The Peter Principle*) called it 'reaching one's level of incompetence', but it has little to do with competence and a lot to do with a mismatch of behaviour requirements and strengths. A key step in creating Best people is helping them understand their preferences and strengths.

If you're thinking, 'Oh no, I don't have to do another personality test do I?', don't worry. There's a simple way to find out if a job suits your preferences. Using the approach we talked about earlier, identify the behaviours that are necessary to create high-level performance in the job and then ask yourself if they are the things you would like to focus 80 percent of your time and energy doing. For example, would you be happy if the critical behaviours were:

- Keep information up to date
- Think problems through logically and precisely
- Make a careful assessment of risks
- Plan things as precisely as possible
- Analyze suggested changes thoroughly before making decisions

On the other hand, if the key required behaviours were

- Take the lead in initiating ideas and actions
- Encourage people to take considered risks
- Get people committed to common objectives
- Generate enthusiasm and excitement
- Challenge people to achieve more

Would that describe a job which suited you?

Generally speaking, we know what we prefer. If you think you are undecided about one of two actions and you flip a coin, quite often you know, while the coin is in the air, which way you want it to end up.

Linking behaviour to performance measures

Talent blossoms when it is given a chance to demonstrate itself. But it rises to its highest level when it is subjected to discriminating appraisal. The audience at La Scala knows Best and refuses to tolerate less than Best. If you want to perform at your peak, you need clear benchmarks. Every good athlete knows what their personal best is, and they know what the world best is. They can link their performance directly to these or other clear benchmarks. Best people need to know how their performance is measured, and they need Best measures – measures set by discriminating experts. Just as getting a round of applause for singing a song in a bar is not the same as getting applause for singing it in Carnegie Hall, having your performance judged on unsubstantiated opinion is not the same as having it assessed against hard, quantifiable, observable, objective criteria.

The example in Chapter 1 illustrates the point. The behaviour of the senior management team was linked directly to the increase in revenues. Once the managers saw the results of their changed behaviour, they became committed to the process. The problem with many behaviour change programmes is that they aren't linked to tangible results.

Coaching and support

There isn't anybody who can't benefit from a coach. Anyone who sincerely wants to improve their performance recognizes this. All the world's best athletes, even though they are at the very top of their professions, have coaches. Why? If they are already better than everyone else in the world, why do they think they need a coach? What can the coach tell them or show them? But

❝ there isn't anybody who can't benefit from a coach ❞

coaches don't have to be better than their client at what the client does; they don't have to know more; they don't have to have all the skills; and they don't have to have all the answers. What they have to do is help their client achieve a higher level of performance. Do you know who Hank Haney is? Few people do. He's Tiger Woods's coach. His golf game can't hold a candle to Tiger's, but it doesn't have to; the effectiveness of a coach is measured by the performance of the client.

Coaching is not therapy, it's not counselling and it's not consulting. Coaching is about helping people change in order to perform better. It's the client who changes, not the coach, and it's the client whose performance improves, not the coach's. One of the core principles of Behaviour Kinetics, the science of behaviour change, is that the starting point for change is acknowledgement of current behaviour – i.e. understanding what one is doing, how that behaviour is perceived, and what its consequences are. The great Scottish poet, Robbie Burns, puts it best: 'O would some Power, the gift to give us, to see ourselves as others see us!' You can't improve your performance until you understand what you are currently doing and what its impact is. All good coaching begins there.

Encouraging ownership and personal responsibility

If there is one lesson to be learned from reviewing talent management programmes, it is that all development must essentially be personally driven. An organization can set a business challenge but then it needs to invite people to respond to that challenge rather than mandating the change.

In the late 1990s, Andrew Curl, Vice-President for Emerging Markets at SmithKline Beecham, created a programme called *Entrepreneur Attack*. Its aim was to tap into the latent potential of the business. The invitation to respond to the challenge of unleashing talent began with the establishment of what Curl called an Enterprise Fund. He invited all his general managers to allocate a percentage of their overall budget to the Fund. They then created a business challenge through which teams in individual operating companies (or several companies combining together) could bid for all or part of the monies to fund entrepreneurial initiatives. These initiatives had to be within certain strategically defined markets, products and service areas, but the rules were deliberately quite loose. As Curl commented at the time, 'We didn't want to create too much process. We wanted to encourage the release of entrepreneurial talent. We did some generic business planning, pump-priming support but just enough so everyone had some guidelines. We then stepped back to see what people could do.'

The results were outstanding. The Emerging Markets division attracted millions of dollars of new business for SmithKline Beecham. But even more importantly, the initiatives helped to unearth, attract and retain talent in all the countries involved. People who had not appeared on the company's radar achieved high profiles. And the programme stimulated widespread informal networking activity, cutting across company, country and functional boundaries.

The process was also transferable into more mature markets. Tweaking his successful formula, Andrew Curl established the Enterprise Risk Fund in SB Europe. Starting with a relatively small fund, the deal was that country operations could bid for funding for projects not financed by their own budgets. Again, projects had to be within strategic areas. If the investment succeeded, then the country operation took half the incremental profit and the Risk Fund the other half, thereby increasing the size of the pot for further investments. If the project didn't live up to expectations, the Risk Fund took the hit. Andrew Curl says, 'It encouraged managers to take risks knowing that they would not have to take any downside. Far from failing, the Fund increased fourfold within a year, backing and benefiting from entrepreneurial activity within a corporate framework.'

Manager to boss behaviours

Threshers, the UK's leading independent specialist drinks retailer, and Boots the Chemist each made the decision to franchise some of their operations. In Threshers' case the decision was to convert their off-licence retailers to franchise ownership. In Boots' case it was Boots Opticians that was created as a chain of independently owned businesses. In each instance an offer was made to incumbent managers to participate in the move to individual ownership. Not everyone found the offer attractive but many did. What started as a move away from corporate ownership developed into a major wellspring of talent discovery and development. In both Threshers and Boots a job behaviour specification was created for owner franchisees. These behaviour specifications were used for both selection and induction and for subsequent development.

If you enable those who possess the capability to operate differently to realize their potential, you get a completely different set of outcomes. Accelerated growth and profitability are the general rule – and they are delivered by the *same* people, with the *same* products, operating in the *same* locations. Corporations are increasingly recognizing the power of freeing people to explore and develop their potential and are beginning to work on ways to bring entrepreneurial types back into the fold, but under new and different terms.

Best people don't occur by accident. They develop when they are given jobs that match their strengths and that lie within their range of preference, and when they have a clear understanding of what they need to do to perform at their best. They need clear benchmarks against which to measure their performance and they need coaching, feedback and support to help them deliver their potential.

This is what a senior manager said to us about creating Best people:

If I had my time again I would not have continually tried to bring in big hitters from the outside as much as I did. I had success on some occasions, but at what cost? They also rarely, on the whole, produced what I thought. Teaching old dogs new tricks just doesn't work. Far better to grow from within and build the talent bank. I wish I had done more of that and promoted from within. There are no silver bullets after all – just an enormous opportunity to tap into hidden talent.

❝ **far better to grow from within and build the talent bank** ❞

Chapter summary

- People perform at their best when they are given opportunities to do jobs that suit both their abilities and capabilities.

- Creating Best people involves a number of actions:

  - Making sure people understand what behaviours are necessary to perform the job effectively.

  - Creating the proper balance between the *what* (clear results expectation) and the *how* (clear understanding of what needs to be done – behaviour).

  - Encouraging self-nomination as a core part of the talent management process.

  - Transferring as much responsibility for performance and development to each individual as possible.

  - Helping people gain an understanding of their strengths and preferences.

  - Linking behaviour to performance measures.

  - Setting up coaching and mentoring processes to underpin talent management strategies.

From a different angle

Healthy culture + enlightened leadership = creating Best people

Enlightened leadership and a strong internal corporate culture result in the creation of Best people. The following suggestions can be instrumental in re-energizing your people and bringing Best to the forefront.

1 **First, understand your old culture**. Understanding the past is nec-essary in managing change and capitalizing on your best talent. Transition to new ways of thinking and performing require an understanding of where you have been and what that might mean within your organization.

2 **Define the culture you want to have**. Culture is about values, shared beliefs, purpose, direction and relationships. The cleanest and clearest definition of organization culture, suggested by Deal and Kennedy in their book *Corporate Cultures*, comes from the former Managing Director of McKinsey & Co., Marvin Bower: 'It's the way we do things around here.' How do you (and should you) do things within your company? What gets people fired up? What are your commitments and relationships with customers? Within your organization, what are your commitments to one another? What opportunities and rewards do you provide your people? Bottom line: Who will want to work for you?

3 **Be highly visible.** As an owner, CEO or key manager, you should be in front of your people constantly. Several companies with whom we are working meet every week – either with their key management or their entire staff – to share the latest developments and to encourage ideas from the staff. High-performance companies have leaders who are very involved in the business of creating Best people by getting them to put forward and develop their ideas.

4 **Listen and build trust**. Building trust begins with a sincere desire to listen. The payoff comes not only from building relationships and trust, but it becomes an excellent vehicle for discovering new ideas and opportunities. Almost every great business leader of today has designed a process to listen to the ideas in the workplace. As Jack Welch, former CEO of GE, says, it's essential to establish a culture where everyone's ideas have value and everyone plays a part.

5 **Build teamwork and a sense of community**. An essential factor in building a strong culture is collaboration built upon teamwork, dialogue, and a strong sense of community throughout the organization. Teams should not merely be at the management level or within a particular department; they should be cross-functional. Set high values and standards with a high-performance culture built around interdependence and team performance, not just individual performance. Best flourishes in a supportive and interactive environment.

6 **Limit hierarchy**. Many companies have restructured and flattened their organizations. This has led not only to cost savings, but frequently to improved communication too. The old organization structure of command and control, of 'manager-as-hero', is outdated. Today's organizational model is fast, flat and flexible. That brings out the best in people.

7 **Define your vision with unreasonable expectations**. In working with successful clients, we have found that leaders who inspire and earn respect can set very high expectations and receive the commitment from their people to make it happen. This defies many planning experts who still preach that goals should be realistic, achievable and credible. In their book, *Contented Cows Give Better Milk*, Catlette and Hadden stress that 'high expectations beget high performance'. In *Leading the Revolution*, Gary Hamel's design rule No. 1 is setting 'unreasonable expectations'. If you want to get the best out of people you need to stretch them; you never know what you can achieve until you try to reach goals you didn't think possible.

8 **Have an understanding where talent lies**. The solution isn't to merely throw a group of employees together. High-performance companies perform a skills assessment to ascertain the skills possessed by each key employee and how those skills (and people) can best be used working with others. They also identify the employees' leadership and managerial styles. The right mix of skills and styles is critical to being able to reach one's best.

9 **Be compassionate**. A study by the University of Michigan Business School revealed that organizations in which employees can describe their companies as 'virtuous' (defined in the study as 'compassionate activity') have a higher level of innovation, customer and employee retention, and profitability. One of our client CEOs is very demanding – setting extremely high expectations – but he also carries out random acts of kindness. He is highly respected, and his staff is highly committed. Caring and kindness mean a lot to Best people, particularly when the level of expectation is very high.

10 **Enlightened leadership**. Your people want to be inspired. They want a vision – to know where the business is headed and the role that they are expected to fulfil. Best in class have strong leadership at the top of their organization, leaders who are visible and stay involved. An organization looks to its leaders for vision, answers, motivation, reassurance and guidance. Leadership best practices include those leaders with a clear vision, who have a sense of urgency, react quickly, embrace change, and have the talent to capitalize on opportunities. These leaders have the talent to create a flexible organization, and they have the sensitivity and people skills to build teamwork and a sense of community.

Creating Best people means getting everyone in your organization involved and excited to participate in the future and success of your organization. High expectations can be set, the culture will be healthy, and high performance will be the result.

Bill Kuhn

Questions to ask yourself

- How much time do you spend on helping your people become Best?
- How much time do you spend on helping yourself become Best?
- How many of your people are deploying their top strengths and enjoying it?
- What could you do to improve this number?
- What would be the impact on the team, you and the organization as a whole of focusing upon this?
- In terms of managing talent, what do you believe you are getting right?
- In terms of managing talent, what do you believe is not going well?

4

How can you keep the Best?

Far and away the best prize that life offers is the chance to work hard at work worth doing.

Theodore Roosevelt

So much of what we call management consists in making it difficult for people to work.

Peter Drucker

Make retention every manager's business

Retaining talented people is much cheaper than recruiting them, but companies continue to accept high turnover rates. And when they recruit new people, they spend very little time integrating them into the organization and training them. According to Deloitte's calculations, American companies spend almost 50 times more to recruit managers at the $100,000 level than they do on training them each year. The simple arithmetic of employee turnover shows a stark picture that organizations seem blind to. Assume a company with 3,000 employees, average salary of £20,000, employee turnover of 20 percent, and turnover cost including the cost of recruiting a replacement of one year's salary. These are conservative figures

> **❝ retaining talented people is much cheaper than recruiting them ❞**

but even so, the cost to the company per year is £12,000,000 and that comes straight off the bottom line. But in addition to all this, what organizations don't seem to understand is that when they lose people, they also lose experience, skill, knowledge and in many cases customer relationships.

There is a very strong correlation between employee retention and the quality of management. The Saratoga Institute conducted 19,700 exit interviews of key employees leaving companies, and found that 85 percent of bosses thought their top people left for more money and opportunity. But the exit interviews showed a very different picture: 80 percent of the leavers said they left because of poor management and leadership or because of a negative and unsupportive company culture (i.e. poor management again).

Is anybody doing anything about this? Virtually every major management and business publication in the world has been running articles about the scramble for talent, but very few organizations appear to be responding to the alleged impending crisis. In McKinsey's 'War for Talent Survey', 93 percent of senior managers who were asked the question 'Should line managers be accountable for the quality of their people?' agreed it was very important. But when asked 'Are line managers held accountable for strengthening their talent pools?' only 3 percent said yes.

It's one thing to identify who your Best people are, but it's another to keep them in your organization. As the great baseball manager Casey Stengel commented, 'It's easy to get the players; it's getting them to play together that's the hard part.' Attracting Best people or developing them is no guarantee that you will retain them. Once talent is identified, it becomes highly valuable and the job market is an open one.

■ In their annual survey of more than 40,000 managers, the Chartered Management Institute and Remuneration Economics found that 7 percent left their jobs in 2006 vs. 4.6 percent in 2005. This prompted the institute's Marketing and Corporate Affairs Director, Jo Causen, to comment, 'If organizations are serious about retaining the best talent, they urgently need to meet the needs and expectations of their staff.'

- A Society for Human Resources Management and CareerJournal.com survey in the US showed that 75 percent of American workers are looking for a new job. The survey showed that 43 percent of people looking for new jobs were seeking higher compensation, while 54 percent were currently dissatisfied with opportunities for growth and advancement in their jobs, with more than half of these looking for better career opportunities.

- A study, 'Is New Work Good Work?' by Andy Westwood for the Work Foundation, observes, 'Evidence suggests that UK employees are becoming more critical of their workplaces, and increasingly less satisfied with what they offer ... More and more workers are dissatisfied with, and the level of (satisfaction) their prospects, pay levels, working hours have all roughly halved in less than ten years.'

Trust as part of culture

For the past 20 years, the Great Place to Work ® Institute has been conducting research into the characteristics of the world's most admired and desirable workplaces. Their findings show that the principal distinguishing feature is trust between managers and employees. They define a great place to work as one in which 'you trust the people you work for, have pride in what you do, and enjoy the people you work with'. But trust, pride in work and enjoyment of working with colleagues isn't something that is industry or country specific. It's an issue of management, not national culture or industry glamour. The top three European Best Companies to Work For in 2007 were Ferrari (Automotive, Italy), 3M (Diversified technologies, Germany) and Abbott Laboratories (Pharmaceuticals, Ireland). In America the top three were Google (Search engine), Genentech (Biotechnology) and Wegmans Food Markets (Food supermarkets)

❝ trust can't be taught; it can only be earned and learned ❞

Trust can't be taught; it can only be earned and learned. Training programmes that purport to develop trust among a group of people by having each one of them fall backwards, eyes closed, into the arms of colleagues don't do much to engender trust in the workplace. Only the most extreme of psychopaths would fail to catch someone in a public and contrived scenario like this. As the faller, you know they'll catch you. The social pressure is so great that they have to. But will they catch you when you stumble at work? Lord Jones, former head of the CBI, talks about the 'brutally competitive' nature of the world of business where, as he describes it, 'India wants your lunch and China wants your dinner.' It's a wonderfully graphic picture, but everyone knows that if you want to experience brutal competition, you don't have to get on an aeroplane to India or China; it's alive and well in your own workplace. At work they might not catch you if you fall, and only the foolhardy fall simply to find out.

How do you know a company is a Best place to work?

The most obvious answer to that question is to look at the level of employee turnover. If it's 30–40 percent as in a number of bank call centres, then one would feel pretty comfortable in saying that it's not a great place to work. But if it's 2 percent, like in Alcon Laboratories (see below), you would have to think the opposite. In a low-unemployment, high-mobility free market economy, if people don't like their jobs, and don't like their company, they get up and leave.

Practising what they preach

Alcon Laboratories, an optical products manufacturer, has about 13,000 employees around the globe. It is a company that is highly attractive to employees. In 2006 there were 70,000 applicants for 87 new jobs. But Alcon doesn't just attract Best. As their employee turnover figures show clearly, they *retain* it.

So what can we learn from them about keeping Best people?

▥ They have created a strong sense of pride among their employees.

▥ They have created an environment where the accomplishments of a single person can affect many in a positive way.

And these aren't just words. They have a Medical Missions Department that donates drugs and ophthalmic surgical equipment free of charge to eye care professionals who volunteer their time to help patients who have neither the money nor the facilities to obtain care. Any ophthalmologist can tell them about a patient who needs eye care and can't afford it, and the company will ship the drugs and/or equipment free of charge. It's a huge source of pride for every manager and hourly paid worker in the company.

Another company that retains the Best is SC Johnson. They have about 12,000 employees worldwide and, like Alcon, a turnover of just 2 percent. It's a family-owned business that makes consumer products – Pledge, Ziplok, Drano, Raid, Windex, Edge, etc. Not as glamorous a business as medical products, pharmaceuticals or IT, but clearly a company that gets it right with their people and that gets it right commercially.

What can we learn from them about retaining Best people? The Chairman and CEO, Fisk Johnson, explains some of the reasons why the company retains its people so successfully.

■ It advocates a culture of mutual respect, fairness, and inclusion.
■ It sets a standard for integrity.
■ It makes being the Best place for the Best people one of its top priorities, not only today but for the next generation.

Size isn't everything

And to demonstrate that size or type of business are not the issues in terms of being able to retain Best people, here are three more outstanding examples: Qualcom (a communications technology company specializing in wireless products and services – 8,500 employees), Nixon Peabody (a law firm with 1,500 employees) and Cisco Systems (the leading supplier of network equipment and network management for the internet – 38,000 employees). While they are very different organizations, the one thing they have in common is a 4 percent employee turnover.

Qualcom's stated aim is 'not to satisfy but to go beyond that – relentlessly and consistently'. There were 80,000 applicants for about 1,400 jobs last year. There is a great deal of pride working for a company that is at the forefront of its business and that constantly strives to do better. Qualcom is one of *Fortune*'s Most Admired Companies. Best people want to be with Best companies, they want to achieve Best results, and they want to be recognized for it and feel proud about it.

Culture is the key to retention

Nixon Peabody is the product of the merger of four law firms but the mergers have not had the effect of unsettling people. The culture has been strengthened. The firm had 8,500 applicants for 56 new jobs last year. It has strong credibility, as evidenced by high rankings among law firms in the fields in which it operates – private equity and venture capital, intellectual property, patent, trademark and corporate contracts. People who work at Nixon Peabody are proud to be there and proud of the firm's accomplishments.

Defining a great place to work

The Great Place to Work ® Institute identifies five dimensions of a great workplace. One of these is what they call *credibility*. Credibility, as they define it, is about managers:

- ▓ Regularly communicating with employees about the organization's direction and plans
- ▓ Asking employees for their ideas and suggestions
- ▓ Making sure employees know how their work relates to its goals and objectives
- ▓ Demonstrating their commitments through their actions

Cisco Systems demonstrates this quality. John Chambers, the CEO, meets all new hires and runs monthly breakfast meetings at which employees can, and do, ask him tough questions and get straight answers. Best people like to work for respected and recognized firms with strong credibility in their industry.

Respect and fairness

Two other rather obvious (obvious to some but for some reason deeply obscure to many managers) elements that characterize companies that people like to work for and give their best for are *respect* and *fairness*.

In the book *Performance: The Secrets of Successful Behaviour,* we talked about a key element of successful change. We called it an AT (Ask Them) approach, as opposed to the more common style of management which is TT (Tell Them). Asking people what they should do to improve performance is far more effective than telling them. As Winston Churchill so nicely put it, 'Personally I'm always ready to learn, although I don't always like being taught.' AT organizations demonstrate fairness by ensuring that everyone has an opportunity to make suggestions, to put forward ideas, to question things. And they demonstrate respect by listening. No emotionally intelligent person expects to have his or her opinions hold sway all the time, but nobody likes to be completely ignored or to have their suggestions denigrated or ridiculed.

> ❝ asking people what they should do is far more effective than telling them ❞

Perhaps the two most famous theories of motivation are Abraham Maslow's Hierarchy of Needs and Frederick Herzberg's Motivators and Hygienes. Both of these eminent thinkers recognized that self-esteem, the esteem of others, and respect and acknowledgement are powerful motivating forces. They are closely linked with the concepts of fairness and respect.

Values – the things that bind or unbind

Injustice, deception, dishonesty, partiality and discrimination all smack of lack of respect and lack of fairness. Quite understandably, people react negatively to them. When they exist, and worse when they *pers*ist in the workplace, people learn to disguise their capabilities and instead divert their energy and attention away from doing their current jobs. Instead they spend time looking for jobs elsewhere. Managers who fail to recognize that it is essential to create a workplace where fairness, respect, pride and openness are dominant values become the creators of what might be termed a 'Best Breakout', where the Best people can leave and do leave.

What do Best people want most in their jobs?

Not all of the companies that get voted Best to Work For are particularly good at managing talent. We're not, of course, talking about attracting a relatively few talented people. What we're talking about is much more in line with what Alcon Laboratories, Cisco Systems, SC Johnson, Qualcom and Nixon Peabody have achieved: the sustained ability to recruit, develop and retain Best people. Hiring high-profile hotshots is easy, but uncovering the gems of talent that lie hidden throughout the organization, getting them to sparkle, and then keeping them as they grow in value requires real management.

The average employee turnover of the 50 top-ranked Best Companies to Work For on *Fortune*'s list is 12 percent. Of these companies, 30 percent have a staff turnover of more than 15 percent. That's the equivalent of everyone leaving in just under 7 years. A number of the companies on the list have a turnover of 20 percent and more. That doesn't say much to us about effective management of talent. It looks a lot like Lawler and Worley's 'travel light' approach, which we discuss further in Chapter 6 – Hire 'em when you need 'em and fire 'em when you don't.

Opportunity to perform

What do Best people want in their jobs? *Principally, they want the opportunity to be able to perform at their best.* Marcus Buckingham's research into what determines high-level performance in companies ('What Great Managers Do', *Harvard Business Review*, March 2005) supports what we know: that the key issue that differentiates high-performance companies from poor-performing ones is whether

❝ they want the opportunity to be able to perform at their best ❞

employees respond positively or negatively to the question 'At work, do I have the opportunity to do what I do best every day?' People who answer yes to that question tend to be Best people. They're the ones who *want* to be able to perform at their peak. From an organizational point of view, the better you manage talent – identify it, develop it, grow it and retain it – the more Best people you will have and the more you will attract. It's the ultimate virtuous circle.

Freedom to act

Baptist Health Care, a company that operates a number of hospitals and health care centres in the US, is an attractive place for people who want to be able to perform at their best. In fact there were almost 20,000 applicants for six new jobs last year. One of the reasons Best people like working at Baptist Health Care is that they are given authority to deal with patient and customer problems directly. Through a programme they call Service Action, when staff at any level identify or learn of a customer problem, they are trained to deal with it within 15 minutes and they can spend $250 to do so. That's the opportunity to be able to perform at your best, and that's why 20,000 people want to work there and why the 4,000 people who do work there, want to stay there.

Retaining Best people starts with the job

Because the principal thing Best people want in their jobs is the opportunity to be able to perform at their best, it's essential they know what they are expected to do. You can't be a Best performer if you are doing the wrong things. We have worked with about 30,000 people over the years, finding out what they are doing in their jobs and whether what they're doing is meeting their needs and the needs of their companies or organizations. In virtually every case of underperformance, we have found that the person's behaviour is not what the job requires. They are doing the wrong things, and because they're doing the wrong things, they're getting the wrong results.

We'll say it again: *Best performers are those people whose behaviour most closely matches the behavioural demands of the job.* To be done most effectively, every job needs its incumbent to do certain things – to display certain behaviours. If you do the wrong things, performance falls. If you do the right things it improves. That's simple, clear logic and we can all accept it. The process we use to identify these 'right' things is described in the example below.

Managing perception and relationships

The common belief is that Performance leads to Results and results lead to success. But performance and results are not enough. There is a second **P** – perception. And there is a second **R** – relationships. The *perception* of performance and the *perception* of results have to be managed. And relationships also have to managed, because the majority of tasks the individual is required to perform cannot be achieved without the cooperation or assistance of others.

All the research on poor performance or underperformance shows that more than 75 percent of the time, people don't know what is actually expected of them. They think they know what they should be doing (their perception of what they are expected to achieve and their perception of what they need to do to reach that target). However, unless they have a good relationship with their manager and other important colleagues where they can discuss what specific results and what behaviours are required, it's a hit-and-miss affair.

Here's an example. A young manager we know moved to a new role in a new company. Her ratings in both her former two companies were excellent. She was (and is) a good manager who produces good results. When she arrived in her new job she started off by doing what we all do – what worked well for her in her last job. But she wasn't sure she was on the right track. The new company was very different from the former one. However, she knew the importance of the second P, perception, and the second R, relationships, and so she immediately asked her boss if he would be willing to discuss his expectations of performance and behaviour.

She and her boss went through the job behaviour specification process we described in Chapter 3. She completed an MCPI Performance Improvement Profile (PIP) questionnaire and her boss completed a job behaviour specification (JBS) questionnaire, the combined output of which provided the following data:

■ The behaviours on which the young manager was *currently* focusing energy and attention and which her boss believed were important for high performance in the job were:
  - Develop plans for various possible contingencies.
  - Try to anticipate people's longer-term reactions to decisions.
  - Strive for consistent performance improvement.
  - Hold people responsible for meeting all their objectives.

■ The behaviours on which the young manager felt she *should be* focusing to improve her performance and which her boss also believed were important for high performance in the job were:
  - Keep focused on the big issues facing the business.
  - Make it clear to people how their performance is assessed.
  - Regularly review how work is progressing.
  - Constantly suggest ideas to increase effectiveness.
  - Help people develop the necessary skills for their jobs.

■ The other key behaviours which her boss believed to be critical for the achievement of her targets were:
  - Provide clear direction for people.
  - Make sure people's ideas and suggestions are recognized.
  - Don't allow people to become cut off from help and support.
  - Encourage people to take reasonable risks to get things done on time.
  - Make sure procedures are helpful rather than obstructive.
  - Create a sense of urgency.
  - Face up to and deal with demanding situations.
  - Set an example by getting change started.
  - State views frankly and openly.
  - Create a passion for delivering more than expected.

You don't know what you don't know

If we look at what the manager was doing and what her boss felt was necessary, a large gap is evident. The diagram below illustrates the gap. As the chart shows, the young manager was currently focusing her energy and attention on coordination and integration of activities and outputs, on short-term objectives and monitoring performance against them, and on implementing and applying system and process. The job requirement, as defined by the boss, was for strong initiative, setting an example and providing challenge to people, while at the same time making sure they are given appropriate support and development.

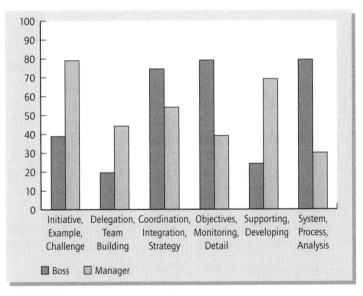

figure 5.1 Comparison of manager's current behaviour and boss's expectations of behaviour

Without some recognition by the young manager of the importance of the second P and R – perception and relationships – she wouldn't have initiated action to make this information available. The meeting to identify the critical behaviours for high-level performance in her job would not have taken place, and the opportunity for her to adjust her behaviour to meet the perceptions and expectations of her boss would have been missed. The probability is she would have floundered in the job and eventually either left or been fired.

Chapter summary

- Organizations that keep Best people:
  - Generate a strong sense of pride among employees.
  - Create an environment where the accomplishment of a single person is recognized and can affect many in a positive way.
  - Set standards around a core set of values such as integrity and fairness.
- The Great Place to Work Institute defined a great place to work as 'one in which people trust the people you work for, have pride in what you do, and enjoy the people you work with'. A key factor in what creates this type of environment and culture is what the Institute calls 'management credibility'. This is all about what managers do (behaviours) on a day-to-day basis:
  - Regularly communicating about future direction and plans.
  - Asking for ideas and suggestions.
  - Making sure that people can see the connections and the ways their work relates to the organization's goals and objectives.
  - Demonstrating their commitments through their actions.

  All of these behaviours can be observed and measured, so great places to work only became so by intent! It's what managers do that makes the difference.
- The resounding answer to the question 'What do Best people want in their jobs?' is principally that they want the opportunity to be able to perform at their best. Retaining Best people therefore starts with the job – Best performers are those whose behaviour most closely matches the behavioural demands of the job.

■ Simply thinking **P**erformance and **R**esults will lead to success is not good enough. Managing **R**elationships and **P**erceptions is equally important to achieving success.

> ### From a different angle
>
> *Managing talent in today's diverse workforce*
>
> My experience indicates that retention and recruiting are two of the biggest problems confronting a company. If you need a wake-up call to trigger action, consider the following:
>
> ■ 70 percent of employees either feel 'not engaged' or 'actively disengaged' in their work.
> ■ Today's workforce will change jobs – even careers – five to seven times in their working lifetimes.
> ■ 60 percent of new jobs will require skills currently possessed by only 20 percent of the workforce.
> ■ Management positions will experience the greatest turnover of any group.
>
> Think about the composition of your workforce and the characteristics and implications typical of each generation (realizing that, like all generalizations, these characteristics do not apply to all members in a group).
>
> *Baby Boomers (1946–64)*
>
> 'Treat them right and they'll be loyal' usually worked, at least for the older baby boomers now in their fifties and sixties. These early boomers usually accept structure and have been the easiest group to manage. The younger baby boomers, now in their forties, tend to be less traditional. But baby boomers in general have a wealth of knowledge and experience, and they tend to be reliable, patient and reasonable. They want autonomy and look for a sense of meaning, in both their personal and professional lives.
>
> But this group is disappearing; many are retiring, often early. Many are less willing, or sometimes just unable, to work longer hours. Others are finding it difficult to keep pace (particularly in technology). Those still working are focused on retirement benefits and health care and they don't

want to see any cuts. Younger baby boomers also have greater financial needs, such as the costs of university education for their children.

Generation X (roughly 1965–77)

Gen X'ers are in their thirties or early forties. A product of smaller families, there are only about half as many as were in the baby boomer generation. Many in Generation X have lost their optimism and become more sceptical. They have experienced recessions, been laid off, faced changing job contracts (e.g. employment at will), and have found themselves over-educated and under-employed.

Unlike baby boomers, they are more independent, less willing to accept structure and constraints, and more willing to try something different. It is estimated that one in five in Generation X is preparing to leave their current job. On the plus side, this generation appreciates a friendly workplace and is beginning to realize that smaller companies can offer greater fulfilment and job satisfaction. In just over 10 years the youngest of them will be nearing age 40, with the expectation that the following 10 years will be their peak earning and spending years. Money will move up the ladder of Generation X's hierarchy of needs.

Generation Y (roughly 1977–97)

Within the next five years Generation Y, sometimes referred to as the Internet Generation, will significantly affect traditional management practices and force some drastic changes. This generation – upwards of 75 million strong – has high expectations and is searching for new ways to define and express themselves. Partly as a function of youth, Gen Y'ers are ambitious, often idealistic and outspoken. They question everything. Self and family usually come first, then friends (including co-workers). The companies they work for often come last on the list. If they don't like a job, they quit. They are motivated by flexibility, achievement, recognition, immediate responsibility, growth and advancement, and money. Without these, they'll move on for a better opportunity.

A new approach is necessary

As you get ready for the challenges of managing an increasingly diverse workforce, there are two key principles to keep in mind. First of all, it's important to recognize that no one approach to motivation and no single set of rules will work today. If you take a 'one size fits all' approach, you risk making at least one and probably two groups of employees unhappy and unmotivated. Second, the talent management system you put in place must be fair and must be seen to be fair. If there are different rules for different groups, the rules that are applied must be equitable – not just for an individual or generation group, but for all within your organization.

That means it may become harder than ever to develop the talent you need – particularly in the context of a highly diverse workforce that varies with age, gender, ethnicity, race, marital status, sexual orientation, values, styles and work–life balance. And even if you do succeed in crafting an effective talent development and retention programme, blending those diverse talents and all the opportunities that each generation offers remains a daunting challenge.

Bill Kuhn

Questions to ask yourself

- How good are you at developing the working environment and culture that your organization needs to keep Best people?
- What is your staff turnover rate and how does it compare with others in / outside the organization?
- How much does *unnecessary* attrition cost your organization?
- Are retention / succession / development objectives part of how a manager is measured and rewarded in your organization?
- How would you describe your workplace culture?
  - What do you like about it and want to encourage?
  - What do you dislike?
  - What isn't happening that should be happening?

Keeping the Best in a takeover
A case study

There is no security on this earth, there is only opportunity.

General Douglas MacArthur

Mergers and acquisitions present a situation where the issues of identifying, retaining and developing the best are placed in high relief. The failure rate of mergers, where failure is defined as inability to increase shareholder value, is above 80 percent. Research studies indicate that about 65 percent of M&As fail due to 'people issues', which are generally lumped together under the heading of 'culture clashes'. Culture is clearly an issue, but to write off all the human issues of mergers and acquisitions under the assumption that a significant majority of people in the organizations involved are unable to alter the way in which they operate is a vast oversimplification and casts a dense fog over much more specific issues. One of these is the retention of talent – retaining people who are strong enough to go but are committed to stay.

The merger myth

❝mergers are virtually never the cooperative act of integration of two equals❞

The word 'merger' is one of those terms that attempt to screen the hard truth about a difficult event. The fact is that mergers are virtually never the cooperative act of integration of two equals.

Boxes in organization charts don't have space for two names. People, mistakenly, are seen by most companies as a cost, and as the profound management thinker and writer Charles Handy remarks, 'If people are counted as costs, then there is every incentive to keep down those costs.' If we cut through the language of pretence and tell it like it is, merger becomes takeover. One party gets to decide who does what and how, and the other side either goes along with it or is removed.

If you read the announcement of virtually any acquisition, the issue of cost reduction is right at the forefront. And in virtually every case there is an unstated (and basically invalid) assumption that the revenues, margins, market shares and the customer base of each party will remain unchanged while various costs will be removed. Revenues and assets remain; costs and liabilities decrease. Who can argue about a deal like that?

Another major unstated assumption is that while costs will be cut, they will all be of the redundant, unnecessary kind and the cost reductions obtained through getting rid of people will be the result of 'cutting out the deadwood'. But how does a company recognize deadwood? And if it is easily recognized, why wasn't it cut previously? Even more importantly, how was it turned from something live and vibrant into something essentially dead and inert? And who or what was the killer? We have to assume that companies don't *recruit* deadwood, so how do these live organisms become fossilized? Taking the wood analogy further, young trees are filled with energy and their growth is a marvellous pattern of branching creativity – just the sort of characteristics organizations want in their people. When we see vibrancy, growth and creativity in people we have a word to describe it: potential. Mergers and acquisitions are great wasters of potential.

Managing transitions to retain the Best

In any acquisition two questions must be asked:

- How do you retain the Best while remaining supportive to those who must leave?
- How do you make sure everyone is clear about what they need to do when structures, roles and cultures are changing?

Many of the transitions we make in life run smoothly and quite painlessly. Others begin with a jolt and are both painful and stressful. The emotional transition curve below outlines the impact of a takeover on individuals, and the psychological and intellectual stages through which they progress as the change takes place. Transition is uncomfortable but the only way to get over the discomfort is to move to the next stage. That's what this chapter is about. It's a case study of how to retain Best people in an M&A situation.

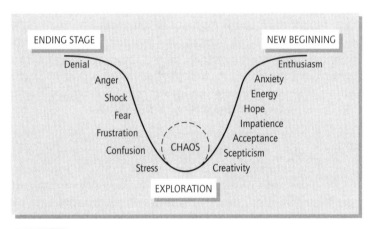

figure 5.1 The Emotional Transition Curve

Managing emotion

The descent into an emotional trough via denial, anger, shock, fear, frustration and confusion manifests itself in stress. Stress is directly related to feelings of lack of control. The people in control of an acquisition don't get stressed; it's the ones who are thrown into the shark pool who suffer from anxiety and insecurity. Chief executives rarely complain of stress until their companies begin to perform poorly and they are unable to turn things around – i.e. they lose control. Individuals engulfed in mergers and acquisitions, even at senior levels, are plunged into great uncertainty; nothing is secure, nothing is predictable, nothing is clear.

> ❝ stress is directly related to feelings of lack of control ❞

The unique role of the line manager

The area at the bottom of the emotional transition curve is characterized by chaos – uncertainty, unpredictability, insecurity, volatility, doubt and instability. The piece in the middle of the cycle is Exploration and it is that part of the process which, if handled appropriately, can do much to flatten the, to misquote John Bunyan, 'trough of despond'. It is where managers with the ability to manage Best can create the tipping point to the achievement of successful outcomes. Unfortunately it is the piece of the process that is often overlooked, and as a result the trough remains and scepticism and impatience become embedded. When that occurs the Best tend to vote with their feet.

Transition behaviours – managing the curve

There are some very straightforward things that can be done to raise morale and to keep a sense of balance. In our work we have observed the things that managers who know how to manage talent and how to nurture and develop Best do.

- They mark the *ending phase* clearly and emphatically by:
  - Stating the implications of change upfront
  - Sharing as much information as possible and maintaining regular contact
  - Providing structure
- They create *the new start* by:
  - Defining new roles clearly (the *what*)
  - Defining necessary behaviours clearly (the *how*)

Failing to address these latter two things as quickly as possible leads to people becoming stuck in the trough of the change curve, mired in increasingly debilitating chaos.

Once people are clear about what they are expected to achieve (job specification) and what they need to do to meet their targets (behaviour specification), 90 percent of the stress and anxiety of change is dealt with. Now they are looking for motivation and direction and managers' focus needs to turn to:

■ Challenging people to action

■ Encouraging personal responsibility

■ Building alliances

■ Celebrating early successes

Management has a direct impact on individual behaviour in terms of effective positive attitude towards change. Retaining the Best under conditions of dramatic change and great uncertainty requires managers to engage issues actively and openly – to take a front-foot stance in dealing with the ambiguities and the insecurities people face. A 'My door is open to everyone at all times' approach is not good enough. The door's threshold is a barrier that even the most senior people fear to cross.

In a recent *Harvard Business Review* article about managing the transitions required when a new CEO arrives, a number of chief executives expressed their exasperation at the reluctance of their senior managers to initiate discussions with them. If very senior managers find the threshold threatening, how much more intimidating must people lower down the hierarchy find it? Individuals who understand how to manage Best know that you have to walk *out* of the door and engage people because the uncertainties, fears and frustrations they are experiencing won't allow them to walk in.

BAT and Rothmans

In January 1999, British American Tobacco (BAT) offered £13 billion ($21.33 billion) for Rothmans International. The acquisition made BAT the second largest tobacco company in the world after Philip Morris, with a 16 percent market share. Shares in BAT rose to a high of £6.75 in January (they were at £2.74 in March the following year). BAT announced expected annual cost savings of at least £250 million from the third year, and a £400 million one-off saving. And so the story begins.

The takeover announcement produced a feeling of shock among the Rothmans people. Rothmans was a highly enterprising culture. Strong family feelings pervaded the business and there was a deep sense of pride at being part of such a highly regarded business with great brands and a strong tradition of sales and marketing prowess. The early part of 1999 saw morale at a low ebb, with an initial vacuum in communications which inevitably affected people as they hit the first few stages of the emotional transition curve – denial, anger and shock.

It's exceptionally rare for an acquiring company to have a complete plan of reorganization ready for implementation, with articulated structures, processes and people clearly delineated. Every merger or takeover has an element of stepping into the unknown associated with it. Due diligence is seldom complete enough to foresee every problem.

> **every merger or takeover has an element of stepping into the unknown**

A principal focus of Rothmans-BAT management was keeping dialogue open, concentrating on day-to-day routines and setting up Q&A sessions, all of which are essential. But it's important to realize that communication alone can never do much more than maintain a tenuous balance of emotions. It helps lessen the uncertainty but it doesn't take it away. The Q&A sessions can't and don't deal with the question that dominates everyone's thoughts: 'Do I get to keep my job?' Unfortunately that question can't be answered until individuals are in possession of clear job and behaviour specifications. Until that happens, much of the organization resembles a multiple-player, large-scale game of blind man's buff.

In the background, of course, there is always a lot of planning being done. Gradually names are assigned to roles and those people whose roles are to become redundant begin to be identified. In the Rothmans-BAT case, this initial phase of planning identified four groups of people:

■ Those who would most likely be staying

■ Those who would most likely be leaving quickly

■ Those who might be offered a role depending on whether a value-added fit could be found for them

■ Those who would go through a transition with a planned exit in mind (6 months / 12 months / 18 months, etc.)

Assessing and addressing the issues

Retention issues loomed large. Who were the critical Best people to keep? What were the criteria for keeping Best people? When Best people were identified, what means were necessary to keep them?

Potential stayers

Of the four groups, the people for whom roles in the new organization were clearly identified and the people who would be offered a role if a fit could be found were the first to be addressed. In order to do this the organization first had to:

- Get individuals to accept some responsibility for determining which roles best met their career objectives and the objectives of the company
- Get individuals to sharpen their awareness of their skills, abilities and experience

Initial conversations with a wide range of people revealed that they had a poor fundamental understanding of their high-value skills and abilities, and as a result a poor understanding of their value in both the internal company and the external job market.

Potential leavers

The other group to which attention had to be paid was those who had been earmarked to leave the company. The costs of redundancy are familiar to all large organizations. They involve cash payments of one kind or another, plus pension benefits and outplacement services and they can be calculated relatively accurately. However, the underlying assumption is that these numbers are basically fixed – that X number of people will leave; that their redundancy and pension payments will equal Y; and that their outplacement fees will equal Z. But this doesn't have to be the case. If the process is handled differently, some of these people in the third group will turn out to have value to add and may be retained, and those that leave will be much better prepared for the outside job market and will require much less time and cost for outplacement.

The alternative approach

On that basis, an alternative approach to the problem was suggested that resulted in a significant saving in the cost of redundancy. The suggestion was to take 50 percent of the budget for outplacement services and apply it to the implementation of a set of processes which were given the title *Developing Your Potential (DYP)*. The principal objective of DYP was to help each individual build what might be termed their personal equity – the understanding of their job/employment value in terms of their abilities (current skills, knowledge and experience) and *cap*abilities (potential). DYP was designed to create the opportunity for an acceptable dialogue about the stay-or-go issue and about areas of opportunity and risk.

By helping people to understand their abilities and capabilities, and by getting them to take responsibility for their career decisions, the process moved from the classical one of selecting, on largely subjective criteria, which people to retain and which people to fire, to one that enabled ability and potential to be recognized both by the individual and the company. The cost saving occurred in two areas: (1) reduced redundancy costs due to (unexpected) retention of previously unidentified Best people, and (2) greatly reduced outplacement fees due to individuals being much better prepared by the DYP process to take on new jobs in the open market.

In parallel with the DYP process, line managers were trained in sponsoring, mentoring and coaching skills and behaviours. This allowed them to better handle the discussion over stay-or-go, and the associated discussion of career potential and development issues. The objective was to create a sense of partnership – manager and subordinate working together to develop a best outcome for the individual and the company.

Put the focus on personal ownership

'Acknowledgement to Action' became the DYP motto. It was recognized by everyone that unless there was acknowledgement of the situation and the issues nothing would happen. There would be no movement forwards – no impetus for personal ownership – no striving to be Best. Acknowledgement to Action was based on the following steps:

- Providing **information** that is helpful to individuals and enables them to form the beginning of personal understanding
- Helping people develop greater **awareness** of their behaviour, skills, abilities, preferences and perceptions
- Getting people to **acknowledge** their situation and the options available to deal with it

This is the link between awareness and action – no acknowledgement, no action. Acknowledgement is the critical turning point where ownership of life and career decisions kicks in and it becomes possible to envision what can be done.

Enable each person to respond positively

The DYP process set out to achieve the following:

1 Help each person to identify and own a career development plan and be in a position to discuss this

2 Focus specifically on an agreed set of behaviours for their roles or prospective roles (behaviour specifications)

Identifying, developing and retaining the Best

Recognizing that the reshaping of the business was going to take some time and that everyone would need support, it was decided to take a phased approach to the way the process would be managed, starting with building support mechanisms for every manager.

Phase 1

Managers were given coaching and support in how to conduct open team meetings, and get-togethers were scheduled throughout the company. Regular bulletins were issued, providing information on the latest decisions and developments. They highlighted successes where these occurred and made public various restructuring decisions and actions, including the movement of individuals into different roles and responsibilities.

There is nothing earth-shattering about these things, but it's astounding how many companies fail to take even these first steps. One of the major barriers to the process is the general lack of coaching and open-discussion-handling skills of managers. These are specific skills that can be learned but they are rarely included in the core training and development needs of managers.

Phase 2

A series of *Developing Your Potential* sessions was run throughout the company. The first task was to help people identify the roles for which they knew they were being targeted, or roles where they believed they could add significant value and felt able to apply for. Once they had a specific job (or in some cases several possible jobs) in mind, the next step was to help them recognize their current abilities, current behaviour, preferences and potential. The final step was to help them to identify the type of behaviour necessary to deliver in these roles.

Phase 3

These sessions focused on how to get people into a better position to sell themselves and to become more confident about their employability and marketability, first in an internal job interview, and, if there was no internal job on offer, through an external interview. The objective was to give people a better understanding of their value in the marketplace. The sessions were about helping people match their behaviour to the demands of their current job, and at the same time to get ready for stay-or-go discussions which might occur as and when the business decided on its future size and structure. To create continuity, people were encouraged to form support groups of four or five individuals who could provide mutual help.

Phase 4

The crossover into this phase came at the point of the stay-or-go discussions. These involved a one-to-one meeting between a manager and a DYP participating individual, and then a subsequent one-to-one for the individual with HR to cover the implications of whatever had been agreed. Just prior to the start of this phase, Career Development Centres (CDCs) were set up in four locations. The role of the CDCs was to provide independent, confidential and practical advice on personal and career issues and to enable individuals to build a range of skills, behaviour and knowledge; to better understand their preferences and to build flexibility; to enhance employability; and to help them take control of their own careers. The following activities were integrated into Phase 4:

- Outplacement support for those leaving
- One-to-one career planning sessions
- On-going coaching
- Release interview workshops

Outplacement support for those leaving

Outplacement support was provided as a key service by the CDC outplacement team. Packages of support varied by grade, but the core services covered the use of all the back-up facilities and research support plus a library of relevant materials and diagnostic support; one-to-one coaching support; one-to-one and group financial advisory sessions; workshop sessions dependent upon needs – job search, self-marketing, self-employment, entrepreneur development, retirement seminars; and top-up career development seminars for those who were not sure of their next step. For those who had already been on a DYP programme, much of the initial preparation work had already been done and therefore their pace during the outplacement programme was significantly quicker and more directly focused on a selected course of action.

One-to-one career planning sessions

For those who had been informed that they would be leaving at some point, the company continued to provide support, but on a phased basis, knowing that six weeks before release date outplacement support would be provided. This helped people grow in confidence and get ready for leaving while at the same time helping them continue to perform effectively in their current role.

On-going coaching

In parallel with the above, everyone who wanted could also have access to a coach to talk about their current performance or work issues. This helped to provide a sense of balance between the 'here and now' and the future.

Release interview workshops

These were one-to-one or small group sessions to help line managers handle giving news of redundancy to their team members. The importance of these sessions cannot be underestimated. Culturally and operationally this is an important moment of truth – a visible test of the values, trust and professionalism of any company. In parallel, the company organized a regular bulletin covering progress and reinforcing a calendar of key events.

The critical elements of retaining the Best in a takeover situation

1   Recognizing that talent is to be found at all levels. The core message was – 'We want to hear and talk through the options that may be possible with you. Where this is not possible, we will support you to become as marketable as you can be.' This focus on guaranteeing quality of process, not on outcome, was practical, realistic and respected.

2   Helping people to think more carefully about who they are, what they want, and how to talk through their strengths and achievements in a realistic fashion.

3   Through an emphasis on self-development and employability, making people much better prepared for the stay-or-go discussion.

4   Maximizing retention. Retention of the Best meant ensuring that everyone who went for an internal job felt committed to stay but, equally, felt strong enough to go. While competency, skill, knowledge, and experience are crucial, when seeking to retain the Best, the most important criterion is best fit of behaviours and values – people who know their minds and want to stay for the right reasons.

By positioning outplacement (for those required through the transition period) as part of the planned exit process, people became more relaxed as they knew support would be there when needed, typically six to eight weeks before leaving. This made it easier to hold the business together as it managed uncertainty. In bottom-line terms, it helped to maintain morale and productivity and to keep the Best. As a result of meeting these commonsense emotional needs, performance improved and managers found it easier to get things done.

A key part of the DYP process was based on Marcus Buckingham's observation that, 'Great leaders tap into the needs and fears we all share. Great managers, by contrast, perform their magic by discovering, developing and celebrating what's different about each person who works for them.' The DYP process set out to help managers build on each person's unique strengths rather than trying to fix their weaknesses. In doing so, it encouraged managers to develop their people by finding the right role for each person.

Chapter summary

■ Explain to managers what happens when change takes place. Induct them into the realities of the change and transition process itself.

■ As soon as possible, provide people with an understanding of what they are supposed to be doing (job specification) and how they need to go about achieving these targets.

❝ initiate a process that looks after both stayers and leavers ❞

■ Help them to understand the emotionality of the processes they are experiencing.

■ Initiate a process that looks after both stayers and leavers.

■ Initiate programmes designed to help everyone:

  - Learn how to sell themselves

  - Learn how to prepare their CVs

  - Learn how to handle interviews

  - Learn how to evaluate offers and choices

From a different angle

Lessons learned in managing a turnaround

Some years ago I was brought in as the corporate CEO for a high-tech client whose operating losses were exceeding gross margin dollars. It proved to be a very challenging experience. Ultimately, the turnaround was successful, and I and my interim management team learned a lot of lessons through an intensely hair-raising, but intensely satisfying, experience. Obviously, many of the issues were related to financial survival, but as significant were the staff members who remained and how they impacted the company's future.

Word of impending disaster spreads fast. Vendors wondered whether they would be paid, customers questioned whether they needed to consider an alternate source of supply, and every last employee was feeling for his or her future. A seemingly inordinate amount of time and effort was spent in scotching rumour and restoring confidence, even when other problems seemed more pressing. One of the best rumours: as I was giving a session on management styles in America to a visiting group of Toshiba executives which included a tour of the plant, I also inadvertently convinced on-looking workers that we had sold the company to the Japanese!

To fight these fires fast and effectively, we had to involve everyone, the entire constituents of the company – employees, managers, directors, owners, vendors, reps, customers, the bank and auditors. While we went about the job of informing, communicating and calming – differently inside and out – the message was the same: we are in trouble, we need your help, we need your best ideas and talent, we have confidence in our future. After all, the best cure for rumour is fact, even when the facts are discouraging.

In-house we faced two distinct problems: employee morale and managers out of harmony with each other and badly shaken by numbers that finally gave a clear picture of previous incompetence.

We tackled the first with hard-hitting employee meetings, encouraging participation and suggestions. I held weekly meetings with all employees on the factory floor. I gave the weekly status report, and said that I would answer any question I could. They listened; I listened. They posed tough questions. 'How many more might be laid off?' My answer: 'I can't tell you, but there will be more staff reductions, and our aim is to keep the best performers and contributors at all levels within the company.' And tough questions to them: 'What's wrong?' 'What's right?' 'What would you do?' A factory worker had the answer. 'You know what? We think we're like a big company, so we're organized on an assembly-line basis. We're not that; we're a high-tech job shop and the plant needs to be organized as such, by customer project.' That saved the day. Productivity improved, quality was restored, and customers began getting their orders on time once again.

Getting management on a positive track was equally difficult. Sad but true – the folks who get a company into a first-rate mess are usually the least equipped to get you out of it. Several key managers had been let go at the very beginning. Those remaining were well aware that their jobs might be in jeopardy because they might be considered part of the problem and ill-equipped to pull together towards a solution. So, of course, we just locked them up and ran a three-day unrelenting managers' meeting. From recrimination and acrimony, to peace-making, to innovative thinking and optimistic planning for the future, by the third day we had a team built to help us with fire-fighting. All of these men and women went back to their own staffs with action plans and a goal to get the best performance and insight from their direct reports that they could. Words of survival replaced words of despair.

We also sought out the ideas and talent of our very best customers: Boeing, McDonnell Douglas, Lockheed, and Texas Instruments. A monthly customer advisory group was formed. Griping about late orders and questionable quality was soon replaced with suggestions and ideas to enable our company and theirs to mutually benefit. The customers were free to leave, as are the employees in an M&A situation. But they liked our product, wanted us to succeed, and helped to bring about that success. No major customer was lost.

In a turnaround, it's people who usually get you into the mess, and it's people who eventually get you out. A turnaround leader can't fight fires alone; it takes a committed team. As the leader, it's asking the right questions and listening, doing everything you can to bring out the highest talent possible. It takes people who display their talents now (not later), who sharpen their skills now, who can make the right changes now.

There was light at the end of the tunnel. The company moved from a crisis stage to stabilization and ultimately to a return to growth. Six months later, the company was again profitable, and improving its financial strength monthly. Ultimately, the company was sold to a major high-tech company at a price that was unforeseen two years before. The company would never have survived without keeping – and developing – the very best talent.

Bill Kuhn

Questions to ask yourself

- How prepared and capable are your managers in terms of managing change and transition?
  - Who do you assess is strong / weak?
  - What can you do to help them?
- What can you do to ensure that you retain the Best?
- Where do you assess the biggest emotional reactions will come from?
  - From specific units? Why?
  - From specific people? Why?
  - What can you do to manage these reactions?
  - What is the best mix of communication actions to take? (Who / where / when / what and why?)

6

How can you recruit the Best?

If each of us hires people smaller than we are, we shall become a company of dwarfs.

David Ogilvy

You're only as good as the people you hire.

Ray Kroc

The **real secret** to getting your recruitment right is to take time to think it through and to understand what the behavioural DNA of the Best people in your organization is. The questions to ask are things like:

- What are the values we're looking for?
- What are the sorts of behaviours that people with these values exhibit?
- What types of reward will these types of people want?
- What are the motivations that drive our Best people and are they what drive the people we're considering hiring?
- What specific behaviours will we require from people in order to enable them to become Best?

This last question is the key to ensuring success. It's not willingness or aptitude or understanding or past experience that creates Best, it's behaviour – *Best occurs when the individual's behaviour matches the behaviour demands of the job.* Once one recognizes that, it becomes clear why so much recruitment is hit or miss.

"you have to know what 10 looks like in behaviour terms" Recruitment needs to be done to a clear behaviour specification. In order to create an organization filled with Best people – people who are doing precisely what they need to do to achieve a perfect score of 10 – you have to know what 10 looks like in behaviour terms. A clear behaviour specification shows that.

Approaches to acquiring talent: 'hire and fire' or develop

In their book *Built to Change*, Ed Lawler and Chris Worley talk about two approaches to managing human capital: a 'travel-light' method and a 'commitment-to-development' method.

Travel light

A travel-light approach means acquiring and discarding people according to corporate needs at the time. Its advantages are flexibility and a constant inflow of people with different experiences and views. Its major downside is the increased risk profile associated with having continually to find talented people. The greater the number of people you have to find, the greater the probability of selecting the wrong ones, and the consequent higher costs of search and acquisition. It is also more difficult to attract talented people with the right skills, knowledge and experience when they know they will be let go as quickly as they have been hired. Loyalty becomes a real issue.

Commitment to development

A commitment-to-development approach gets to the heart of managing talent effectively. First of all it implies measurement. Talent cannot be managed successfully unless the skills, abilities, experience and adaptability of people can be calibrated. This is far more difficult to do when you have no working knowledge of individuals. The travel-light approach, based on a continuous flow-through of new people, means that you are always working in the dark when you're assessing individuals' potential. The system makes it exceedingly difficult, if not impossible, to create meaningful measurement of ability or capability. The best you can do is live in hope that you will 'know talent when you see it'. But with a commitment-to-develop system, where your people are at hand and readily observable, it is relatively easy to get an accurate measure of people's skills, knowledge and ability.

A commitment-to-development approach implies creating what American sports teams call a 'farm system' – a system of teams at different levels of skill through which players progress. It's a cultivate-your-own talent system and is common in most of the sports world. But theatre companies, orchestras, the armed forces and the established churches also work under the commitment-to-development approach. There are back-ups, understudies and clear steps for succession in all of them. What makes business organizations think they are different? What makes a great many of them pay scant attention to succession planning? Less than 25 percent of companies have identified internal successors to key roles below the first couple of levels. Why do they feel they have to scour other companies for talented managers? What message does that send to their own managers? And for that matter, what message does it send to shareholders?

Internal versus external hiring policies

There are obvious advantages to bringing people from outside into an organization. They tend to arrive unburdened by prevailing ideas and systems and find it easier to adopt new approaches to existing situations and problems. But there is also a great deal to be said for knowledge and understanding of how the people and systems in the company work, and for established networks of strong relationships with people across the company, to say nothing of longstanding relationships with key customers and suppliers. Procter & Gamble have maintained a policy of promotion from within for many years. They hire people from outside as well, but there is a very clear and well-defined succession plan and career path at P&G. Coincidentally it happens to be one of the 'great' companies identified by Jim Collins and Jerry Porras in their book *Built to Last*. P&G knows its people, knows their abilities and has a decent handle on their potential.

There are a number of reasons why relatively few organizations adopt a commitment-to-development approach, but the principal one is that it requires consistent focus and it takes time. And consistent, sustained focus is not a characteristic shared by many managers. Unfortunately there is a (largely unnecessary) pressure for action in most companies that drives people to opt for the hoped-for short-term solution. Mignon McLaughlin's aphorism springs to mind: 'There are so many things that we wish we had done yesterday, so few that we feel like doing today.'

How do you predict future performance?

A number of years ago one of Rank Xerox's top priorities was hiring quality salespeople. The decision was made to focus on recruiting female teachers who were getting tired of teaching and wanted to do something different but something that was still challenging and interesting. The principal driver of change for these people was disenchantment with teaching, but the recruitment effort (called the 'Annie Oakley Initiative' after the famous sharp-shooter who worked with Buffalo Bill in his Wild West Show) specifically targeted women who also had a financial motivation.

The rationale behind the initiative was that, being trained teachers, they had proven skills in communicating, and in preparing and presenting. They also had experience in handling difficult people and difficult situations, although not in a formal selling sense. The issues this campaign raised are central to the whole process of recruiting Best people. Can potential be identified? What are the criteria for successful identification of specific roles? Does success in one field or role predict success in another?

> **does success in one field or role predict success in another?**

The Annie Oakley Initiative was a resounding success because while talent is situational, it was able to identify a set of key behaviours that were common to both the role of teacher and the role of salesperson. This meant that teachers who exhibited these behaviours appeared to have the potential to handle selling roles. We know that experience in one role doesn't necessarily mean success in another, but if we go back to the lists of things we identified in Chapter 3 that help create Best people, they also all apply in the case of identifying potential.

■ **Create a behaviour specification for the job.** Once you have a clear set of the behaviours that are required, you can test people in simulated situations and see if they are able to demonstrate the behaviours effectively. And you can train them in these behaviours.

■ **Create a system of self-nomination for the job.** The advertisements for the sales jobs were targeted at female teachers but, by definition, those who applied were self-nominated. It's quite a career change from teacher to salesperson and only those who believe they have the potential are likely to put themselves forward.

■ **Transfer responsibility for decisions, actions and results.** Sales is one of the areas of business where measurement is relatively easy. All other elements being equal – same product, same pricing, same marketing support, etc. – it's the behaviour of the salesperson that makes the difference. Responsibility for getting sales sits squarely on the salesperson's shoulders.

■ **Select people whose strengths and preferences fit the job.** There are a number of common identifiable characteristics of people who enjoy selling products like copiers. They include being able to take rejection in their stride, being tenacious, etc. People whose preferences are not to be placed in conflictual situations, not to be subjected to criticism, and so on, are not likely to be happy in sales roles.

■ **Link behaviour to performance measures.** That's simple – effective behaviour (i.e. as in the job behaviour specification) leads to good performance (level of sales), while inappropriate behaviour (i.e. different from the job behaviour specification) leads to poor performance.

■ **Provide coaching and support**. That goes without saying, but many companies fail to do it. They put people into jobs and let them flounder. Kevin Howes has something to say about that later in the chapter.

How it has been done successfully

Roger Philby, CEO of Chemistry, an innovative search business and consulting company, was formerly head of recruitment at Energis, now merged with Cable & Wireless. Energis was a company that was taken from insolvency in 2002 by a group of banks who owned the company's debt. Energis was a telecoms company operating in an industry where the sky was falling in, competition was fierce, and the owners, sitting on about £700 million of loans, were not feeling particularly patient. Roger's job was to attract people to the company to help turn it around. He began by making an assessment of the situation and the environment in which recruits were being asked to work. Here, in his words, is how he describes the process:

What will people be walking into?

We started our thinking from the business end – what was the environment? What best characterized the world in which our people were having to live?

- Ambiguity was everywhere; no day was the same; priorities changed hourly.
- Pace of delivery was beyond rapid; a year-long objective had to be delivered in three months.
- Change was the norm – the only one.
- You were judged on what you delivered.
- Feedback was frank, honest, but brutal.
- Pressure was relentless.
- A manager was expected to make quick decisions.
- Planning was not valued.
- 80 percent was OK except when it wasn't ... but you never knew when it was or when it wasn't.
- Everyone was dealing in a customer service environment where nothing less than 99.9 percent was acceptable.
- The business was under-resourced with no cash to staff up to 100 percent.

How will new hires have to behave?

In order to determine the performance behaviours of Energis Best People, we asked ourselves some key questions: What did the organization value? How was this mirrored in the behaviours that were rewarded or thwarted? A great example was in the area of planning and project management. Planning was something not valued at all at Energis. In order to succeed, you had to be able to deliver and plan simultaneously. You couldn't stop to reflect and contemplate your next move, there was not time. If you valued planning then you couldn't join. It was that simple.

So what does your organization value? For example, does it value honest feedback? If it does, that's great. However, this will require certain behaviours that need to be developed across all those in your business who have feedback responsibilities. Are you going to take the time and put the effort into developing the behaviours relevant to doing this well? This is the recognizable, observable and measurable nitty-gritty of making sure that people demonstrate the behaviour that the organization values – how stuff gets done. The important thing is to put whatever you say you value into an everyday observable and measurable language. If you don't underpin values in this way, how can you know if they are being lived up to?

Motivation

Then we looked at motivation. What type of person would be attracted and motivated to work in Energis? People who worked well at Energis were motivated by non-hierarchical structures, autonomous decision-making and being part of an intellectually challenging peer group. People who liked structure, hierarchy and set goals and boundaries for decision-making did not perform well. Performance accelerators were motivated by Energis. People whose behaviour focused more on sustaining performance often found the company less comfortable.

The questions asked of applicants were: What do you value and find motivating? What behaviours would best exemplify these values? An example of a response is: 'I value feedback. The behaviours that response implies are that I will ask people to tell me precisely how my performance is to be assessed, what behaviours are deemed critical to achieving my objectives and what those objectives are. And I will ask to be told regularly, not sporadically, how I am performing. I will listen carefully, discuss openly and agree on both my targets and my progress towards them. And I will focus my behaviour on the things that we have agreed are necessary for me to be successful. I want to see the people who work for me exhibiting these behaviours as well.'

The Best profile

The answers to these questions allowed us to define what people needed to look like in order to be Best. The behaviours that defined Best in a majority of jobs were centred on accelerating performance – i.e. on driving change, on achieving a vision, on increasing effectiveness, on driving things forward. We turned all this analysis into a three-stage process for identifying Best people amongst applicants.

Where are they?

First we asked the question: 'Where are these talented people? Where would we source them from?' The surprising answer was 'Anywhere'. We had broken the War for Talent myth. The issue was not what people had done but *how* they had done it and what environments they had done it in. Energis had redefined the rules of engagement; they had taken the war to the competition's backyard. We hired from the FMCG, financial services, consulting, aerospace and automotive sectors. There was no shortage of people to select from because we had shifted people's thinking about what Best was about.

How do we stimulate interest in us?

The next questions we asked were: 'How can we get the talent interested in us? How can we attract the people we want?' To answer this we created an Employee Value Proposition which we could put to people. It went like this:

- Do you want to work in an environment where people will be smarter than you?
- Do you want to work in a place that is broken beyond understanding?
- But where the strategy is clear and you will be able to personally impact the business up or down by 20 percent every day?

- It's not a career move; it is two three year project where you will learn more than you would have done in the last 10.
- Oh, and you may well make some money from it.

What is your organization's employee value proposition? Is it compelling enough to win the hearts and minds of the talent you're seeking to attract? Is there a clear blueprint for the behaviour of the

> **what is your organization's employee value proposition?**

people you need to drive the business forward? Does everyone within the business – your line managers and HR professionals – ask these questions? Is your message, in terms of the way you source and attract talent, communicated seamlessly throughout your organization and through your whole supply chain – your suppliers, advertisers and recruiters?

Which people will fit best?

The final question that we asked was 'How do we know which people to hire?' The approach was simple: put the bar high, and don't compromise. We used assessment centres because they allow critical and important behaviour to be observed. We also used behavioural event interviews designed to probe, with the focus on evidence, how people achieve results. And we used intellect and values screening.

In summary this is the process we used:

Take the time to define what the DNA of your Best people is. Ask yourself what environment you have; what you reward, motivate and encourage? How do your current Best people behave? Create the template; define what 'great' looks like in a way you can observe and measure, and that means in terms of behaviour.

Create a sourcing strategy that works for your Best people template. Where could these people be found? Are they in the competition? Or, actually, could they be anywhere? Create a story and build it into a candidate proposition ... then educate, educate ... suppliers, advertising copy, managers, every possible touch-point. Create a robust and consistent selection process. Gather as much data as you can. Look for the necessary behaviours every time. Trust the data. Don't compromise.

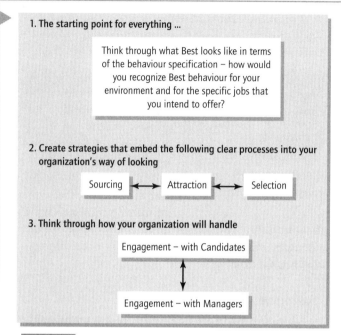

1. The starting point for everything ...

> Think through what Best looks like in terms of the behaviour specification – how would you recognize Best behaviour for your environment and for the specific jobs that you intend to offer?

2. Create strategies that embed the following clear processes into your organization's way of looking

Sourcing ⟷ Attraction ⟷ Selection

3. Think through how your organization will handle

Engagement – with Candidates

⟷

Engagement – with Managers

figure 6.1

Remember the template for your Best people is fact. If the data don't support the decision to hire, don't hire ... the cost could be 14x the base salary. Brad Smart, in his book *Topgrading*, has calculated the cost of a mis-hire at 14x base salary. Whether you believe the rate is 14x or 5x, it's still a large figure.

The Chartered Institute of Personnel & Development estimates that 75 percent of all hires are mis-hires. In their Human Capital Survey, PricewaterhouseCoopers found that 90 percent of senior appointments failed to live up to expectations. The CIPD have calculated that £5 billion of management time each year is wasted on the recruitment process. That's £5 billion to get three out of four hires wrong!

To get recruiting right you have to spend time. Marcus Buckingham says 'Time is non-negotiable. You will spend the time. The only question is where you will spend it; on the front end, carefully selecting the right person, or on the back end, desperately trying to transform the person into who you wished he was in the first place.' The traditional recruitment process is, as Tom Peters would say, broke, and it needs fixing.

Roger Philby

Linking recruitment with actual management practice

How do you help new recruits hit the ground running? Most failure takes place in the first 100 days on the job. Individuals who haven't made the successful transition to their new job in that time, who haven't established the necessary relationships with the people and groups that count, haven't worked out what the culture rewards and punishes, and haven't identified how to add real value within that time period, tend to live on borrowed time subsequently. Here's an example of how to ensure these things are avoided. It's how Kevin Howes, a consultant colleague of ours, handles the merging of an individual into a new job.

The Kevin Howes' process

Step 1 – environment

The first stage of the process is relatively standard. It involves a briefing about the following types of things:

- Products and support services
- Opportunities, threats and priorities for the business
- Sources of sustainable competitive advantage
- The culture of the business – what it values and what it doesn't
- The key stakeholders, including bosses, peers, staff and customers
- The key people with whom the new manager needs to build a relationship
- Areas from which to expect support
- Areas from which to expect resistance

Step 2 – profile Best

The next stage involves using the *Momentum CPI Performance Improvement Profile* (PIP) to do two things: (1) to establish the behaviours the candidate used to create success in his or her most recent job – i.e. prior to being considered for the new role, and (2) to create a list of the key behaviours necessary for success in the new role – a behaviour specification. Here's an example of the top ten success behaviours identified for a new commercial director of a manufacturing company:

- Take the lead in initiating ideas and actions.
- Get people committed to common objectives.
- Set a standard of performance excellence.
- Put specific performance criteria against corporate targets.
- Provide clear feedback to people on their performance.
- Ask people to identify what they need to do to make a difference.
- Insist on regular and open discussion of successes and failures.
- Commit people to clear delivery targets.
- Encourage risk-taking and personal development.
- Enlist the support of key players before tabling an issue.

A behaviour specification gives a very clear picture of what the job is about. This isn't a general description of some competencies, nor is it a job description listing responsibilities. It's a crystal-clear plan of action: if you focus your energy on doing these things, you will be successful in the job.

Step 3 – match behaviours

The next step is to meet with the candidate to discuss the differences between this list of behaviours and the behaviours on which he or she had focused in the previous job. This highlights the necessary behaviour transition. This is the type of performance coaching in which a number of sporting coaches engage. It looks at what the individual did to get to his or her current level of performance and then what is needed to move on to the next level. It works as well for managers as it does for athletes, but it's something that few managers consciously and purposefully do when they change jobs – or even when they are considering changing jobs.

Step 4 – align goals

Once there is understanding about the behaviours needed to make the individual successful in the new role, the discussion can be moved forward to deal with the issue of how each of them is linked to the role's goals and objectives. This is a key step. It's one thing to know what one is expected to achieve and how one is expected to behave, but it's absolutely critical to understand how these behaviours link to the job's objectives – how and why doing X results in Y.

For a new manager coming into a role for the first time, the identification of the behaviours deemed essential for success – the behaviour specification – and how they link to what he or she is expected to achieve in the role, is gold dust. This also provides the new manager with another rather useful view of the company's culture – i.e. what behaviour is considered Best and, by default, what behaviour is not. Very few new hires get this type of information. Instead they go into their new jobs virtually blind and have to feel their way along to discover how Best is defined. It's rather like a rat in a psychologist's maze. If it chooses an incorrect path, it gets an electric shock. If it chooses a correct path, it receives a food pellet. Eventually the rat will find its way through the maze, but not until it has had quite a few shocks. The rats tend to continue to try to find their way through to the end of the maze but humans are less shock-resistant and after a number of shocks they are often inclined to do what Peter Drucker calls 'retiring on the job' – i.e. they give up the idea of adding value and just go with the flow.

Step 5 – stakeholder analysis

The final stage of the process focuses on the relationships with key people inside the organization and with key clients. This is done in the context of the business priorities and the related expectations for the new manager. The reality of any job is that there are a number of different stakeholders. These include the boss, peers, subordinates, individuals in related areas of the business, and key customers. If, in order to achieve certain goals and objectives, a manager needs to enlist the cooperation of one, two or three individuals or departments, it's very useful to know who these people are and a little bit about them.

Conversations with key figures in the hiring organization can help identify where the new hire needs to develop relationships. With a little bit of extra homework, one can also discover where the new hire can expect most support and where he or she should expect resistance. If this diligence is conducted well, it will also be able to identify the sort of behaviours that will resonate best with each of these key individuals – i.e. how to approach them, what they expect, what they value and what they dislike. Even the most rudimentary information is helpful. Early successes make life much easier for a new hire.

The output of this process is a series of action plans set out in three segments of 30 days each, that is, a draft 30–60–90–day success agenda. Each action plan contains the four or five specific behaviours required to create necessary momentum towards achieving the basic objectives of the role, and it contains a list of the most important relationships that need to be established and what specific behaviours are most likely to further those relationships.

The CIPD barometer of HR trends and prospects, 2007, noted that 69 percent of businesses have trouble retaining talent, and around 50 percent of organizations have no formal resourcing strategy. When it comes to filling job vacancies, 82 percent of businesses report they have difficulty. Part of the problem is that when organizations do recruit people, they fail in the first three months to give them the necessary information and support to perform their jobs effectively. That is when they are operating

> **66 69 percent of businesses have trouble retaining talent 99**

under the full glare of attention and any errors or mis-steps are magnified. 'How is the newcomer working out?' is a question frequently heard. Some people hope that the answer will be positive and some, for a variety of reasons, may hope it will be negative. None are provided though with a structure for actually helping the individual to navigate the minefield that is so apparent to insiders but almost invisible to newcomers.

Chapter summary

■ Predicting future performance — the six points made in Chapter 3 apply equally to the identification of potential.

■ The Energis example illustrates three major elements in successful recruitment of Best people:

   - Be clear on what Best behaviour looks like in your culture and organization and for the specific jobs you intend to hire people into.

   - Create strategies that embed clarity into how the sourcing, attraction, selection processes need to work — in the context of your market.

   - Think through how your organization will handle the two-way engagement process between the 'receiving' line manager and the new hire.

■ The Kevin Howes example illustrates a process for the successful recruitment and selection of a new senior hire:

Step 1: Set the context / situation brief with internal stakeholders to establish the role specification and objectives.

Step 2: Establish the behaviours the candidate used to create success in their most recent job and then create a list of the key behaviours necessary for success in the new role (job behaviour specification).

Step 3: Interview 1 — to discuss behaviour match.

Step 4: Interview 2 — to discuss behaviours in relation to the new role's objectives and expectations.

Step 5: Interview 3 — to focus upon relationships with all the key stakeholders.

Are you prepared to recruit the Best?

Most companies report increasing difficulty in recruiting talent. A recent independent research and advisory service, Bersin & Associates, conducted a survey on the subject of talent with 700 US organizations that included interviews with 60 HR executives. They found that two of the three top talent challenges that were identified related directly to recruiting: (1) gaps in the leadership pipeline and (2) difficulty in filling key positions.

While businesses like to say that 'people are our most important asset', when it comes to recruiting and selecting (or for that matter, keeping) talent, the process is often unsophisticated and little different from it was decades ago, frequently with disappointing results.

Reality test

How good are your recruiting skills and those of others in your organization who are involved in the selection and interview process? If you want to find and keep the very best people that you can, you'd better be able to grade yourself and others involved in this function as a 9 or 10. Unfortunately, our firm more typically sees a 5 or 6 in terms of competency and in the techniques involved in recruiting, interviewing and selecting.

What priority does your company assign to attracting (and retaining) talent? If the priority is high, it means you are committed to the process of training – improving recruiting skills and interview techniques, reference checking and assessment methodology. It also means that you have adequately identified the behaviour and skills you need.

Does your company have a positive culture that is attractive to potential applicants? Culture matters to the entire workforce – baby boomers, Generations X and Y, male and female, young and old – who are seeking the right organizational culture to satisfy their personal and professional goals. Strong cultures are performance driven, built on a sense of community and trust. Unhealthy cultures lack a sense of vision, standards of excellence, and strong support values (such as integrity and trust). They are often fragmented or just plain dysfunctional.

Finally, have new and creative approaches to recruitment been tried to meet the needs and desires of talented applicants you wish to hire?

These are a few of the questions I ask clients. The answers often show just how little attention and importance companies really assign to recruiting; they are more likely to harp on how tough the labour market is and how the talent pool is shrinking.

Essential aspects of preparedness

Make hiring and retention a big deal

If recruiting and developing talent is a major concern and challenge – and it should be – you need to include human resources at the heart of your strategic business plan. It should be incorporated into your goals, strategies and opportunities, and not merely as tactical action plans. Re-evaluate how you hire, develop, retain and reward your talent. Invest in HR training, including recruitment, communication skills, and the understanding of today's workforce, its desires and requirements. The additional cost will be more than offset by higher performance and lower turnover.

Evaluate your current recruitment and staffing practices and whether you are using the best recruiting sources. Recruiting must be supported by staff who are skilled in HR management and by highly qualified recruiters. Every person involved in staffing should know what to look for among applicants (including talent) and be able to explain to any recruit where the company is headed and the opportunities that exist.

Assess your culture and market your company

A healthy culture is essential in attracting and keeping best talent. Can you describe your culture and would your best talent describe it the same way? Identify gaps between the atmosphere you would like for your employees and what currently exists. If improvements need to be made to strengthen your culture, work with the talent you have towards that improvement.

Assuming a positive culture, a company should market itself and its culture to potential applicants in ways similar to how it markets its business to attract customers. The key in marketing to customers is differentiation; it's no different for talented applicants. Marketing – branding – your company provides both a customer and a potential applicant a frame of reference. Develop creative 'job' marketing that attracts candidates with something more exciting than a job description or employee handbook. Tailor your jobs to the talent you're seeking rather than fitting the person to the job (yes, this is the opposite of past theories).

Look internally and consider your people and their hidden talents

Stated another way, you need to re-recruit your top talent, providing them with opportunities for learning, growth, advancement and reward. A prerequisite is knowing where your talent and potential talent lie. You may decide in a particular situation that additional learning and development of existing talent is better than hiring an unknown outsider. And remember, if you don't re-recruit your talent, other recruiters and competitors may do it for you.

Develop creative approaches to recruiting

Some recent successes in recruiting approaches have included team interviewing, engaging more of your people in identifying and seeking talent (getting your right people talking), or providing innovative cafeteria plans – each employee has different hot buttons – such as flexible work schedules, time off, working at home part of the time, varying compensation programmes, or programmes for learning and developing new skills. One client identifies his three 'I's'of recruiting: imagination, inspiration and innovation.

New approaches mean thinking outside the box. I have worked with a growing organization whose business is based upon establishing franchises around the world. Its recruitment approach: target talent within major corporations and offer those people a franchise/owner opportunity. It doesn't require much travel, it's one where they have the control to manage and balance their work and personal lives. Those franchise openings have become quite quickly filled with good talent.

Will you take the steps necessary to recruit best talent? Companies with a strong culture, that invest in human resource professionals, and are smart enough to identify talent and 'close a sale', will capitalize on talent opportunities that most companies will miss.

Bill Kuhn

Questions to ask yourself

- How good is your organization at attracting and retaining the talent you need?
- Does your organization have a positive culture that is attractive in the market?
- Does it have a First 90-Day Programme for all new hires?
- Do you take account of the *what* and the *how* (behaviours) in your preparation?
- Do you explore the future factors for success as well as past job successes?

7

How can you make Best job changes?

No person is your friend who demands your silence, or denies your right to grow.

Alice Walker

The most successful people are those who are good at plan B.

James Yorke

The modern work environment is characterized by a high level of personal change. The average individual makes more than three career changes during their working life and statistics show that people in the Western world have an average of about 14 different jobs between the ages of 18 and 34.

The term 'career path' is misleading. It gives the impression that there is a clear progression from first job to final job; that it is just a matter of following a series of steps. But there's a lot more to it than that. Job change involves a transition from one set of skills to another, from one set of relationships to another, and sometimes from one organizational culture to another. It's new bosses, new colleagues, new objectives, new resources, new sources of support (or lack of it), new measures, new rewards and new pitfalls. Managing job changes is like navigating a boat through swirling currents, hidden shoals and alternately calm

ᏨᏨ managing job changes is like navigating a boat through swirling currents ᏗᏗ

and stormy waters. We call the skill of successfully managing job change 'transition navigation'.

In the 1990s one of us was involved in an outplacement programme for Lloyds TSB Bank. As the bank restructured its operations, 500 bank managers were made redundant and went through a programme to help them find outside employment. The assumption was that these 500 branch managers did not have the talent to take on other roles at the bank. They were thought to be at the end of their management careers.

Everyone was tracked in terms of what they decided to do after they left the bank and the results were fed back to senior management at a special *500 Review*. During the presentation one of the slides summarized the career options that people had selected. It showed that around one-third had gone on to start up and run businesses and that most of the rest had quickly found other jobs.

To the HR director and his team this proved almost inconceivable – 'Put that slide back up! Is that correct? If it is, how much in line are we, or not, with other companies? What does this tell us about our culture and operating style?' Everyone found the results surprising in the light of their assumptions of the 500 individuals. And they agreed that the bank's internal appraisal/development processes and systems had not picked up on any of the skills, knowledge and potential that the people in the group clearly possessed. How many potential Best people were lost? The figures appeared to indicate at least several hundred.

Capability – often only understood when it has left

This isn't a unique Lloyds' problem, it's a widespread phenomenon. And the reason is that organizations are bad at recognizing the second part of talent – *cap*ability. They tend to have blinkers on when it comes to being able to see what people could do differently. Does your organization have a section in its performance appraisal where a judgement is made about an individual's potential? How many times have you seen people's careers effectively shut down by the comment 'Lacks potential for advancement'? On the other hand, have you *ever* seen a box which is headed 'What the individual thinks he/she could do to add value'?

The culture of Lloyds, like the culture of most organizations, had created a certain pattern of behaviour. Lloyds' policy was to hire young people (aged 17–20), provide them with incentives to conform to certain types of behaviour, give them a great mortgage package and offer them the chance to become managers. But one of the underlying elements of the culture emphasized keeping one's head down, not creating any waves, etc. People showed the bank the behaviour they believed it wanted to see, rather than showing it what they were capable of doing (i.e. their potential). As long as the status quo was maintained, this arrangement suited both parties. However, when conditions changed and the employment arrangement was terminated, all bets were off and people were free to rethink and rediscover themselves.

Organizational culture determines how people perceive what is possible, how they assess risk and opportunity, and what behaviour is appropriate. While working at Lloyds Bank, the 500 took a number of decisions, formally and informally, consciously and unconsciously, to play their lives and careers out in a particular way. They showed the bank and, in particular their immediate managers and teams, the behaviours and attitude they felt were required. There was a level of what appeared to be comfortable collusion, but in fact the 500 were simply trying to match their behaviour with their perception of the behaviour requirements of their jobs. They were attempting to be Best, as Best was defined by the bank. The problem was that the bank had allowed an underlying culture to deceive the managers into believing that conformity to unwritten behaviours was an actual behaviour specification.

Why do organizations find it difficult to recognize potential, to develop it and to manage it? And why is it that very often individuals find it difficult to exploit their talents? There are a number of traps that can, and do, stunt personal and career growth. But there are some practical things that can be done, on both sides of the table, to encourage the effectiveness of transition navigation in personal and career situations.

Limiting beliefs

Limiting beliefs have everything to do with perception and generally very little to do with reality. Organizations of all kinds, commercial and non-commercial, fob off responsibility for limiting beliefs by attributing them to various social factors that supposedly exerted their effects long before the individuals got into the workforce. Insecurity, lack of confidence, lack of self-esteem and self-respect, risk aversion, reluctance to take initiative, etc. are all put down to early life experiences with family or education and nothing to do with treatment at work. But the fact is that organizations play a massive role in creating and reinforcing limiting beliefs. They are very good, often unwittingly, at sapping initiative and creating conformity. Lloyds is only one example of thousands.

“ organizations play a massive role in creating and reinforcing limiting beliefs ”

Robert Dilts, who has written widely on coaching and change, puts forward an interesting model about limiting beliefs. It helps to explain a lot of the dynamics at play in the Lloyds 500 example. It springs from the phrase 'I can't do that here'. Think of the Lloyds example as you go through Dilts' explanation of how each of the words in this sentence acted to limit the members of the 500's belief in themselves.

- **I** has to do with our feelings of identity, self-worth and self-esteem.
  (Limiting belief: 'I was a young person who was lucky to have got this job. I don't have experience.')
- **can't** has to do with our beliefs and values.
  (Limiting belief: 'The bank has been good to me and I should repay that generosity by doing what they expect of me.')
- **do** is related to our skills / knowledge.
  (Limiting belief: 'I have limited skills and knowledge and those I have I got from what the bank has taught me.')
- **that** is related to our behaviours.
  (Limiting belief: 'I have got to where I am by behaving this way and behaving differently would put all that at risk.')

■ **here** is related to environmental factors which we believe don't allow us to act and achieve something.

(Limiting belief: 'Creative thinking in a bank is a euphemism for fraud. The bank has systems, processes and procedures that have been put there for a reason and you mustn't violate them.')

The antidote

High-performance managers understand limiting beliefs and do various things to overcome them. They give permission to people to try new things and learn; they offer encouragement but also give specific advice and guidance on how to improve performance; they give frequent feedback; they try to allocate the right tasks and projects to the right people at the right time; they specifically look for opportunities to develop individuals' strengths, stretching and enhancing capability. In short they help people become Best.

Hijacking transitions

Stephen Covey, author of the highly readable and helpful book *The Seven Habits of Highly Successful People*, takes an interesting view of the issue of limiting beliefs. He says when we are born we grow up in a family environment and are *dependent*. As we grow and develop and become more mature, we become *independent* and are therefore able to stand on our own two feet. The next stage is that we become *interdependent* – i.e. we are able to mix and interact maturely with many groupings and learn to manage relationships that are central to becoming Best.

However, very often a hijack occurs that diverts people from becoming independent and makes them what we term *co-dependent*, a state where they become cocooned by the organizational culture, as in the Lloyds 500 example, and screened from the realities of what needs to be done to manage their lives and careers. The resultant dampening of personal responsibility manifests itself by depressing potential.

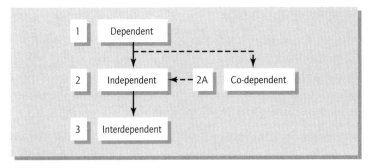

figure 7.1

The dangerous thing about co-dependency is that while it takes on the appearance of being a safe option, in reality it is an untenable position because situations constantly change and if you can't adapt to the change, you're sunk. A former Chief of US Army General Staff, General Erik Shinseki puts it rather well: 'If you don't like change you're going to like irrelevance even less.' The problem with co-dependence is that, in effect, you give the power to control vital elements of your life to the organization, you give up the ability to make change decisions independently, and you consequently put yourself in a position of vulnerability when the company decides to make changes.

Our research shows that it is not possible to go from position 2A (co-dependence) to position 3 (interdependence) in one step. New skills, knowledge, understanding and confidence need to be instilled first. The pathway requires moving back from co-dependence (2A) to independence (2) and then progressing from there to interdependence (3). This journey is what transitions navigation – the development and practice of the skills involved in successfully moving through a job change, career, or life stage to another – is about. It is the art and science of ensuring that each person in the business is self-aware and controls their own destiny, and that they have the requisite knowledge, skills and behavioural understanding to manage transition successfully. As Cliff Hakkim puts it in his book, *So We Are All Self-Employed*: 'The biggest mistake any one of us can make in our lives is to think we work for someone else.'

Beware incremental change

The requirements of a job change almost daily, even though the job title remains the same. The great problem that results is that, because the changes are small and incremental, they remain below our radar until one day, having accumulated significant mass, they loom up like a towering iceberg.

A number of factors affect how careers progress. Unpredictable events can accelerate or decelerate the rate and direction of change. Individuals' personalities and risk acceptance profiles affect their reactions to opportunities and threats. The level of planned support that is targeted at people at different stages of the career cycle can make a big difference in how careers are managed. Things like secondments, assignments and time off work to complete qualifications are important levers that aid in successful career development. Talent management processes have to be a combination of bottom-up initiatives – encouraging individuals to step forward and be ready, willing and able to discuss their motivations and aspirations – and top-down, with organizational programmes and initiatives which make it possible for managers to engage in open discussion about jobs and career aspirations.

What are the secrets of successful transitions navigation?

1 Creating and maintaining relationships

Establishing and maintaining relationships, generating trust, building rapport and influencing outcomes give individuals a huge advantage over people who pay inadequate attention to relationships. The ability to create influence, network, get air-time with the right people, know when to take the lead or not, and when to make sure behaviour is in step with significant others, enables people to handle job moves and role changes with ease.

2 Building enterprise approaches

The way in which individuals behave with regard to opportunities, how they see potential, and how they do things to move towards it and make it happen, shapes their approach to transitions. Seeing opportunity and making the effort to take advantage of it differentiate those who move successfully through their working life from those who experience major dislocations from time to time.

3 Reaction to risk, learning and change

Being receptive to change, prepared to adapt, and being open to learning enables individuals to achieve a better balance between opportunity risk and opportunity failure. Approaching situations wide-eyed and without regard for possible inherent risk is not a formula for career success. But on the other hand, neither is it helpful to overestimate risks and shy away from initiative.

4 Creativity and innovation

Questioning the rationale for processes, systems and decisions, and generating ideas and suggestions for how something might be improved or changed for the better opens the mind to the issues of role and behaviour transition. It takes you 'outside the box' and allows you to think about different and perhaps better ways to do things. Anyone who works in an organization that discourages this type of thinking is setting themselves up for a fall.

5 Self-awareness

A key component of successful job transitioning is a high level of self-awareness. How can you change if you don't know what and where you are to begin with? Self-awareness enables people to make better judgements about their future. It enables individuals to better answer the question 'What does successful behaviour look like in this role, and can I handle it?' One of the most important results in the Rothmans example we

> **self-awareness enables people to make better judgements about their future**

talked about earlier in the book was that a number of people recognized that they were in jobs that suited them and they didn't wish to, or need to, move to something else.

What are the traps in managing job and career transition?

Trap 1: co-dependency

Getting into the co-dependency position and not recognizing it, or recognizing it but not doing anything about it, is the most common trap. It is a life in limbo, neither heavenly nor hellish, comfortable but not exciting, but as we have seen, not as secure as it appears. Staying too long in a job or role without challenge or change causes skills to become stale and outdated and steadily erodes one's value in the open market. It also steadily destroys self-confidence. It kills the ability to be Best.

Trap 2: over-dependence on sponsor(s)

Having sponsors is clearly very useful but watching out for yourself is critically important too. Tying one's career to a star is great as long as the star remains in the ascendant, but if the star crashes, as they do from time to time, and the tie is too strong, there is no escape. The tie is too strong when one's behaviour becomes moulded by the sponsor's wishes and expectations and not by the actual demands of the job. In this case losing a sponsor can leave an individual tremendously exposed.

Trap 3: the 2Ps and 2Rs

We've talked about the second P – perception – and the second R – relationships – earlier. When we start our working lives, we typically win through on our technical and functional skill sets and the behaviours that produce the results; performance and results are closely linked. We become noticed as having 'talent' and the organization then wants to see more of what we can contribute.

There comes a day when we are given our first major, visible role or first management role. It's now that we need to become aware of the importance of managing perceptions and relationships. Bringing five new major account customers to the business can be perceived as a significant achievement or just as something that is expected. Expectations shape perceptions and need to be managed. The old maxim is to underpromise and overdeliver. And relationships are critical to success because the majority of things cannot be achieved without the cooperation or assistance of others.

How can you embed the principles of transitions navigation in your business?

SC Johnson, whom we mentioned in chapter four, created a programme in 2006 called My Work / My Life. It was the first time that the business had sponsored a programme where the focus was as much on life as it was on work. Why did they do this?

Encouraging self-reliance and self-determination

SC Johnson believes that the balance of these two elements is important in terms of increasing employee engagement, and that increased engagement leads to greater productivity. My Work / My Life helped employees analyze how much time they spent on various tasks such as emails, training meetings and product development. It also helped them assess how important each activity was to business unit goals, individual goals, customer goals and other standards important to the business. Once they had a full picture of how much time they spent on various activities, employees were able to take steps to reduce or eliminate the time spent on minimal value tasks so they could concentrate on high-value-added activities. This sorting of priorities had the added benefit of allowing individuals to manage the balance of their home life and work life better.

The SC Johnson principles of empowerment, engagement and involvement are all part of the maturity process that transition navigation involves. The recognition that first and foremost people work best when they are engaged emotionally is the chief element in systems of successful transition navigation. Helping people identify personal and business goals and affording them the opportunity to talk these through with their managers creates engagement and involvement.

> ❝ people work best when they are engaged emotionally ❞

There is a need within all organizations to create a common language in which Best can be defined and this, as we have said, should be in terms of behaviours. What do you want people to *do*? As well as giving them a job description/specification, can you give them a behaviour specification? Behaviour fit is the starting point for any organizational process dedicated to encouraging the release of potential. Behaviour specification for every role must be the basis of recruitment, selection, induction, training and development, and talent management processes. Everyone in the business needs to be absolutely clear about what they have to do (behaviour) to perform well and to be in a position to release their potential.

Chapter summary

- There are five main elements to successful career transition:
  - Creating and maintaining relationships
  - Building enterprise approaches
  - Reaction to risk, learning and change
  - Creativity and innovation
  - Self-awareness

■ There are a number of traps that need to be avoided when navigating and managing a career:
  - Co-dependency
  - Over-dependency
  - The 2Ps and 2Rs
  - Linking one's future too closely to the success of someone else
  - Limiting beliefs

■ Raising self-esteem, building confidence and skills, and encouraging personal responsibility for learning and development are specific activities that enable successful career navigation.

From a different angle

The importance of building a succession management programme

My writings and workshops have typically focused on strategic planning and leadership development, emphasizing their direct correlation. I now add a third component: succession planning or, more appropriately, *succession management*. All three require that you address the skills and qualities that your business has and that your business will need in the future – getting the right skills in the right place at the right time.

This was brought home to me at a strategic planning retreat I was facilitating. The client principal – a highly enlightened visionary and pace-setting leader – surprised us all by suddenly asking his managers a series of questions: 'Who wants my job in the future? Why? And if not, why not? Are you prepared to take it today? What additional leadership qualities and skills do you need to take my position?' This resulted in a half-day discussion, and proved to be the most important part of the two-day planning retreat. And now, upon reflection a year later, the team's performance has been absolutely outstanding in terms of growth, market power, profits, leadership and several internal career transitions.

As the CEO of your company, have you come to terms with the fact that one of your primary responsibilities is the development and cultivation of the future leaders of your organization? Do you have a programme of succession management and an exit strategy for yourself? These actions are critical whether you plan to sell or keep the company.

Begin by asking and answering two fundamental questions:

1 **Where is the business going?** Answering this question means spelling out purpose, a well-defined vision, and the direction the company will take. This question also lays the foundation for and emphasizes the importance of professionally managing the business for either management succession or an outright sale.

2 **Who has or may have the skills and leadership abilities to get the business where you want it to be?** Answering this question requires an assessment of your employees' existing leadership qualities, behaviour and performance. It also means evaluating characteristics including awareness, self-confidence, a strong desire to achieve, a sense of urgency, and the abilities to inspire, empower, establish trust, earn respect and execute.

Once you've answered these questions, set your criteria and objectives for business perpetuation (management succession) or for a sale (ownership succession).

Management succession objectives should spell out an orderly transition based on performance. While all the details of a succession management plan may not be communicated to everyone, the plan should not be shrouded in secrecy. Key players need to know where they stand; openness, honesty and dialogue are essential components.

If sale to an outside party is a consideration, your key players will again influence the outcome. Shareholder value includes goodwill, which is heavily influenced by your people and their performance. Under either succession alternative (whether you keep or sell your business), planning for income continuity, enhancing goodwill and maximizing shareholder value are important objectives.

Focus on development

To enhance value, you must commit to learning, development and understanding. Succession planning is not merely identifying promising employees and the slots they might fill. The focus should be on developmental activities, combining training and real-life exposure. Stretch your staff by increasing challenging roles and assignments. Successful examples I've seen include broadening roles, switching roles, dropping some functions and taking on others (often unrelated). One successful CEO client purposefully takes extended vacations as one method of leadership development, insisting that he can only be reached in an emergency ('and had it better be an emergency!').

Identify your successors

For years, I followed the basic premise of identifying successors early in the process, followed by their development. There are times when this may be required, but my experience has now shown that best practices typically result when the focus begins with development. In due time, the role to be filled by a successor, and the qualifications and strengths required in a potential successor, will become a key staffing decision for which you are prepared. Keep in mind that any good plan includes not only those being groomed for succession, but also the people who will replace them.

Continually monitor performance

Measure progress regularly and evaluate the on-going performance of your key personnel. Ascertain whether the right people are moving into the right positions at the right time. Determine which jobs within your organization are most critical to achieve the vision and direction you desire, and identify any shortcomings in your leadership development and succession management.

Bill Kuhn

Questions to ask yourself

■ Have you identified successors to all your key team/organizational roles?

■ What does team/organizational success look like for you?

■ What is the prize for getting this right?

■ What is the cost of getting it wrong?

■ What does your organization do to build the skills of effective career management?

■ What are you doing to encourage self-development in your organization?

8

How to kill talent

I find it rather easy to portray a businessman. Being bland, rather cruel and incompetent comes naturally to me.

John Cleese

All stressed out and nobody to choke!

Bumper Sticker

What are the things organizations and managers do that stifle talent, that drive it away, that destroy it and that wantonly waste it? What does managing talent badly look like? We know a lot about how to kill talent but nobody seems to want to address the issue, even though the costs are immense.

Up to now we've been talking about how to manage talent well. But because we know that it is *not* often managed well, what is the flipside of the process? You won't find a lot written about that. But if you want to be able to identify, develop, recruit and retain Best people, it's rather important to know what you should avoid doing. People and organizations don't seem to want to acknowledge doing these things, probably because they see them occurring frequently, and in many cases collude in them.

Toxic management

The most conservative estimate of the cost in the UK of what Jeff Pfeffer calls 'toxic management' is estimated at about £20 billion a year. That's the figure from the UK National Workplace Bullying Advice Line. If data from the CIPD are used, the figure moves out of sight. A Roffey Park Management Institute study of 500 managers, quoted in the *Daily Telegraph* in January 2008, showed almost 70 percent of public sector managers reporting bullying in their workplace, along with 42 percent of managers in the private sector.

The effect of targeted toxic behaviour on one individual cuts their work rate and effectiveness by 50 percent. Witnesses to the behaviour and co-workers of the targeted employee have their work rate and effectiveness cut by about 35 percent. That makes the estimated average cost of a single manager's serial toxic behaviour about £70,000. A US example is quoted later in the chapter. It calculates the cost of a top-performing salesperson's toxic behaviour at $160,000.

Charlotte Rayner and Loraleigh Keashly have studied the costs of toxic behaviour in the UK and their finding is that 25 percent of people who are the targets of this behaviour, and 20 percent of the people who witness this behaviour, quit their jobs. The Roffey Park study confirms this. It shows 66 percent of junior managers and 56 percent of middle managers saying they want to move out of their current jobs. Rayner and Keashly have done some arithmetic to show the monetary cost, purely for replacing these people, and not including the cost of lost productivity. They have come up with a conservative figure for an organization with a thousand employees of about one million pounds a year, straight off the bottom line.

It's what managers do on a day-to-day basis that counts

We've had more organizations than we care to count tell us that they need to recruit new people because the ones they have aren't good enough. If this is true, and they continue to recruit 'good' people and get rid of 'poor' people, when will they reach the point where they have dispensed with all their poor performers and are now staffed with nothing but good performers? If a bank call centre, with a 40 percent turnover rate and an estimated annual recruitment cost of about £50 million, keeps flushing out 'poor' people and replacing them with 'good' people, that should mean that after two and a half years they shouldn't need to recruit anyone else. The large banks claim to be highly effective and extremely sophisticated recruiters. They use batteries of predictive instruments which they claim to have rigorously tested and validated and they employ allegedly advanced interviewing techniques. So why, after a 30-month flush-out of 'poor' performers and an intake of carefully screened 'good' performers, do they continue to have the same turnover rate? We're just using banks as an example because they have high staff turnover in various segments of their business and are high in the public eye. But they're not alone in this. The problem is endemic.

The argument that 'Our people aren't good enough and we need to continually recruit better ones' simply doesn't stand up. If everyone in the company was a poor performer, then it would have failed long ago. If 20 percent weren't up to scratch, then a relatively brief recruitment campaign and a focused development programme should have solved the problem. The fact is that much of the time it's not the people in the organization who lack talent; it's their managers who don't know how to manage it.

Talent is far easier to stifle than to grow. The educational system is notorious for suppressing creativity and original thinking in children, which is perhaps why so many highly successful entrepreneurs did poorly at school and left before continuing on to higher education. Billionaires Richard Branson and Philip Green left school at 16. Mary Kay Ash (Mary Kay Cosmetics) and Debbie Fields (Mrs Fields Cookies) started their businesses when they left school. Michael Dell dropped out of university at age 19 and Bill Gates dropped out at 20. Albert Einstein's remark comes to mind: 'The only thing that interferes with my learning is my education.' Organizations have unfortunately adopted the educational model. They call it command and control. It's an adapted version of 'sit in your seat, face the front, be quiet, and listen to what you're told'. And it doesn't work.

> ❝ talent is far easier to stifle than to grow ❞

Talent and good management go together

The amount of talent that exists in an organization is directly related to the quality of its management. Good management attracts and keeps Best people, and bad management drives them out. This is an irrefutable fact. If you look at the 2007 *Fortune* list of the ten Least Admired Companies, the correlation is confirmed. If we take innovation in an organization as an indicator of the success with which it manages talent (and innovation occurs when people are given freedom to express ideas, are listened to and supported – i.e. managed well), the numbers tell the story. On a scale of 1–15, where 15 is worst, the average innovation score for the ten least admired companies is 12, and their corresponding scores for overall quality of management is 11.

Thinking about the various ways in which managers and organizations suppress talent brings to mind the opening line of Elizabeth Barrett Browning's most famous sonnet, written for her husband Robert Browning: 'How do I love thee? Let me count the ways'. Can we count the ways people's talent and potential are blocked? Probably not all of them because the list is rather long. You will no doubt have examples and if you'd like to tell us about them, then we'd like to listen (and we've given our email address to do just that) because encouraging, helping and supporting people to be the best they can be is of the very highest importance, not just in terms of organizational performance, but in terms of pure humanity and decency. Stripping people of the opportunity to fulfil their potential verges on the criminal.

Blocking Best

Holding people back

In July 2006 the Institute of Leadership and Management (ILM) conducted a survey of 6,500 people aged 18–24, in full employment. The results were not encouraging. One-third said their managers did not allow them to contribute ideas or suggestions; another third said they were told to do things without explanation, a quarter said they thought they could do their manager's job better, and 11 percent said they felt their manager was holding them back. Currently, more than 400,000 people in the UK, aged 18–24, believe they are being held back by their managers.

Fear of being surpassed

There are, of course, a wide variety of reasons why managers and supervisors hold people back. One is the fear of being surpassed by someone who has greater ability, drive or capability. However, one of the marks of a good manager is the ability to identify talent, and to grow and enable it. The inscription on Andrew Carnegie's tombstone reads 'Here lies a man who knew how to enlist in his service better men than himself'. The insecurity and defensiveness that leads people to fear having others around them who know more than they do, have more ability than they do, and have greater potential for advancement than they do, is a powerful force that motivates them to maintain their fragile self-concepts. Really good executives surround themselves with good people, without worrying about anybody showing them up. That's one of the distinguishing features of a great leader. Robert Goizueta, the late CEO of Coca-Cola, put it rather well: 'There's no limit to what a man can achieve as long as he doesn't care who gets the credit.'

Fear of losing valuable resources

But managers often hold talented people back because they don't want to lose them. Because they believe in the fiction of a War for Talent they think that, if they let a top performer move on, they won't get anyone else to fill the gap. Often these people leave anyway, so the manager is no further ahead. If, however, managers created a reputation for developing people and helping them progress their careers, they would be inundated with people wanting to work for them and their value to the organization would multiply. Talent-growers are hard to find and are worth their weight in gold because they create a lot of gold. While the goose's golden eggs have value, they are nothing compared to the value of the goose that lays them.

One way to grow and protect golden goose talent-growers is to reward them significantly more than talent-suppressors or talent-killers. The performance measurement is simple: it's based on the number of people who, having worked for a manager, move on to perform successfully in other jobs. One of the greatest examples of a talent-grower is Archie Norman, former Chairman of Asda and Energis. The list of people who have worked for him over the years includes John Pluthero, Chairman of Cable and Wireless, Andy Hornby, Chief Executive of HBOS; Allan Leighton, Chairman of Royal Mail; Richard Baker, former CEO of Boots; Paul Mason, CEO Levi Europe; Justin King, Chief Executive of Sainsbury's; and Ian McLeod, Chief Executive of Halfords. The list is much longer but the point is made. There are more than 20 chief executives of major European firms who have worked for Archie Norman. He's the absolute opposite of a talent-killer.

Not linking performance to behaviour

Organizations are (sometimes) good at setting clear performance targets. They are generally poor at linking these targets to behaviour. One of the recognized weaknesses of annual performance appraisals as they are commonly conducted is that they focus on the past. As Shakespeare so nicely puts it, 'What's done is done and cannot be undone.'

The supposed point of performance appraisals (apart from determining reward) is that people hopefully learn from experience and perform better next time. However, there is a flaw in the reasoning. It assumes that the individual understands what he or she did (behaviour) to achieve the results, and, more importantly, knows what should be done differently to improve them. This is the central issue of the book *Performance: The Secrets of Successful Behaviour* – that in order to improve performance, people have to know those two things, and that it is the duty of managers and companies to find a way of helping them get that information.

Here's an example of the top five things a regional general manager in an FMCG was doing to deliver on his objectives:

1   Helping people learn from their mistakes.
2   Separating broad policy goals into manageable objectives.
3   Helping people develop the necessary skills for their jobs.
4   Helping people realize what they're capable of achieving.
5   Making sure procedures are helpful rather than obstructive.

Timescales and managing expectations

How can these be the wrong things to do? They're all about getting the best out of people and they all create and support accomplishment. They tend, however, to take a longer-term view of performance and as it turned out, the CEO and the board had a different perspective. Here are the top five behaviours which they believed would be most important in delivering the results they expected:

1   Carefully examining the consequences of all decisions.
2   Making a careful assessment of risks.
3   Making it clear to people how their performance is assessed.
4   Providing clear direction for people.
5   Requiring people to commit formally to plans and objectives.

These behaviours talk to a perceived need to act more carefully, to be more considered, to be more cognizant of risks, and to tie people down to clear goals and objectives. They are a top-line version of the behaviour specification for the job of this particular regional manager.

Unfortunately, being told what the CEO and board wanted at an appraisal interview at the end of the year wasn't much use. What a waste of time, not to mention a waste of a year's effort, energy and resources. The general manager left the company. He learned that he needed to get the behaviour expectations set out clearly right up front next time. The CEO and board learned nothing: they simply recruited another GM and hoped for the best.

The killing talent formula

So if you want to kill talent, don't tell people what they need to do to perform their jobs well. Don't give them any sort of behaviour specification for the job. Just let them fumble around trying to work out what they need to do to deliver on their performance objectives, and when they fail to reach their targets, make sure they get the message – they're failures.

Low social intelligence

A potent set of talent-killers are the behaviours that are demonstrated by people who have what Daniel Goleman terms 'low social intelligence'. Social intelligence is a combination of social awareness (understanding other people's thoughts, feelings and intentions) and social facility (behaving and interacting appropriately). If you don't have any understanding what other people are thinking, what they're trying to do or trying to communicate, and you don't understand the emotions behind their actions, the way you react to them becomes a hit and miss affair. By the same token, if you don't understand the effects of your actions on others, you have no way of measuring their impact, positive or negative. Social intelligence goes hand in hand with emotional intelligence – understanding and managing one's own emotions. Low levels of social and emotional intelligence have disastrous consequences in organizational settings.

Toxic talent

The term 'toxic talent' was coined by the originator of the website *Flip Chart Fairy Tales,* who goes under the nom de plume 'Rick'. Here is what he says:

There are people in most workplaces whose behaviour costs their organizations large amounts of money. The toxic manager makes everyone else's life a misery, thereby increasing staff turnover and lowering the morale of those people who decide to stick it out. Tackling these office psychopaths is not only morally right, it makes economic sense too. In my experience though, the really annoying toxic individuals are those who perform well against whatever criteria are being used to measure people at appraisal time. I have worked for a number of organizations where appalling behaviour was excused because the perpetrators brought home the bacon.

In one company, a maverick executive had created a highly profitable line of business. He was considered to be untouchable and his overgrown-toddler behaviour was tolerated and even indulged. His habit of throwing laptops or pieces of furniture across the office in response to some minor frustration was just laughed off. After all, it's what these clever creative types do, isn't it? But there is also a cost to this behaviour. The nervousness of the employees who have narrowly missed being hit by a flying laptop is bound to have an impact on their performance. I like to illustrate the problem with a bar chart.

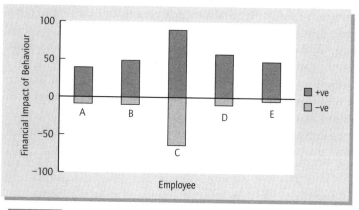

 Toxic talent

In this example, Employee C contributes the most to the company's revenue. He would therefore probably get the highest bonus. What his bosses don't take into account, though, is the impact of his negative behaviour. When you subtract that from his performance figures, Employee C is the worst performer in the team. Allowing for the cost of this bad behaviour, C's performance is way outstripped by D's, who has brought in less revenue but has not cost the company money through being a toxic talent. Rather than rewarding C with a bonus, the company would gain more financially by tackling this behaviour. However, very few employers are willing to step up to such a challenge.

Here's another example, drawn from Robert Sutton's book *The No Asshole Rule*. In this case, the company took creative and effective action to deal with the behaviour.

Although he was consistently ranked among the company's top five producers, Ethan was a toxic manager. He routinely belittled his colleagues, bullied his staff and sent out abusive emails. Eventually his behaviour became so bad that no-one in the company would apply for jobs in his team. His reputation seemed to have spread to the outside world because HR struggled to fill the vacancies, even after an expensive external search.

After warnings and training had little impact on Ethan's behaviour, his boss lost patience. The company worked out the cost of Ethan's despicable behaviour and deducted it from his bonus.

- Time spent by Ethan's direct manager: 250 hours valued at $25,000.
- Time spent by HR professionals: 50 hours valued at $5,000.
- Time spent by senior executives: 15 hours valued at $10,000.
- Time spent by the company's outside employment adviser: 10 hours valued at $5,000.
- Cost of recruiting and training a new secretary to support Ethan: $85,000.
- Overtime costs associated with Ethan's last-minute demands: $25,000.
- Anger-management training and counselling: $5,000.

Estimated total cost of asshole for one year: $160,000.

Still, the company was magnanimous. Ethan's boss only proposed to deduct 60 percent of the total cost from his bonus. Predictably, Ethan flew into a rage and blamed everyone else then threatened to quit. But his managers held their nerve and Ethan was left with the choice of changing his behaviour or continuing to pay what they term the 'asshole tax'.

The goal of the toxic manager

The question people who work for toxic managers always ask is why? Why do they do these things? Is it just for the pure enjoyment of it? Is it because they had a deprived childhood? Is it in the genes? Does the devil make them do it? The answers are: partly yes, no, no and no. The goal of domineering, bullying, demeaning, belittling, intimidating behaviour is just what those words imply – to make people feel inferior to the toxic individual.

There are hundreds of psychological 'explanations'. We put the word explanations in quotation marks because there is some doubt as to the validity of some of them. We don't pretend to have any greater insight than others, but having listened to what a number of very knowledgeable people have said, and having worked with a few of these toxic types, the picture seems pretty clear. In every case we've come across, the behaviour of the toxic individual is covering up a fear of inadequacy. This often defies all logic. We know individuals whose achievements and successes are staggering but who still feel they have to abuse people to assert their dominance and superiority. Their skills, abilities and knowledge are such that people would willingly follow their leadership if they simply behaved normally, but they feel compelled to bully, browbeat and intimidate in spite of this.

Toxic talent, as Rick so excellently describes it, is really nothing more than bullying. Every bully you have ever met had a low self-concept and felt insecure and the reason they bullied others was to keep them from recognizing it, or, far worse, challenging it. Once they were challenged, they melted like the wicked witch of the west in *The Wizard of Oz*. The bully works on the basis of making you feel inferior in some way, either physically intimidated or threatened in some other manner. In an organizational setting, they often get away with it because they control the fate of those who they bully and their behaviour is not recognized (or is ignored) by people above them.

> **toxic talent is really nothing more than bullying**

So if the toxic individual's goal is to make you feel inferior – and hence to allow them to do whatever they want on the basis of being superior – there are various ways to deal with the problem. If you know you have ability and capability, you can leave and go and work somewhere else. Jobs in the Western world aren't the same as the gulag. You don't *have* to do anything. There are always alternatives.

If you're really resilient, you can let the behaviour wash over you and pay no attention. As Eleanor Roosevelt said, 'Remember, no one can make you feel inferior without your consent.' This is an 'I can't change things so I'll pay no attention to it' approach. It takes a lot of self-control and it requires a robust personality not to let the denigration get to you. If this is the route you take, just make sure you keep repeating Eleanor Roosevelt's remark to yourself.

Tackling toxic management – change the learning

However, the behaviour can be dealt with. Toxic behaviour is not personality, it's learned behaviour. Essentially all behaviour is learned. If one learns, in whatever manner, that one can assert superiority over people, bully them and intimidate them and get away with it, one is more likely to do so. But if you change the learning experience for them, you can change their behaviour. You can bet Ethan's behaviour changed after his painful bit of learning.

Chapter summary

- The concept of toxic management is not new and estimates of its impact are well documented.

- Toxic management always costs money! The collateral damage is also often only revealed after the person has gone.

- Tackling this is never easy but is essential in order to create and safeguard the working environment needed to attract and retain Best people.

How to go about losing your Best talent

Research studies abound as to why Best people leave their companies and some of the major reasons are listed below. None of these will come as a surprise to anyone, but what organizations fail to acknowledge is that people are more apt to stay when the opposite of these things is true.

- Unacceptable pay and benefits
- No sense of belonging or having real friends at work
- No clear sense of company vision and direction
- Little pride in the company and its standards
- Little respect and trust of management, including one's supervisor
- A lack of exciting and meaningful work, no job satisfaction
- No new challenges or potential for growth and advancement
- No empowerment and little autonomy
- Little recognition and appreciation
- Limited flexibility and freedom
- Lack of work–life balance (leading to burnout)
- Company's stage of evolution incompatible with individual's needs

Evolution of a business

The last of these reasons is perhaps the least understood, but it is a major factor in causing talented people to leave. The evolution of a business was first described by Larry Greiner. He identified five stages of growth (creativity, direction, delegation, coordination and collaboration). Each stage typically involves a dominant management style. The stage begins with a period of evolution, progresses through a revolutionary period of management and organization turmoil, and (hopefully) ends with successful resolution of the crises. If it doesn't, the company never gets to the next stage, and ultimately dies.

As we have collaborated on some projects, we have found the stages of growth a defining factor in the ability to lose (or keep) Best people. It is essential for leaders to understand the reality and consequences of their own evolution, and the impact one stage has on the entire workforce, compared to a different stage. Sadly, many leaders really don't comprehend that what 'was' is not what now 'is'.

In stage one, there is excitement in the new venture and lots of challenges (including survival). People know one another and there is often a sense of camaraderie. Pay may be modest and the hours may be long, but if there is hope for the future, Best people tend to remain. Stage one's crisis is typically one of leadership; a strong manager is necessary to evolve into the next stage, and founders may be unwilling to step aside. If Best people believe the company will remain small, they will move on.

Stage two is characterized by directive leadership, growth, more formal systems and specialized duties. Again, the question of leadership comes up: leaders may not have mastered the art and skill of delegation, creating a crisis of autonomy, and this state of affairs can lead to good people leaving. Some managers are good at running a $10 million company but not a $25 million one, while others can handle a $25 million company but not a $50 million operation. The main driving force of stage two is growth − often a fast track − which can be both good and bad. More opportunities open up, with growth fulfilling many of the desires of Best people. But fast-track growth by itself isn't enough and the factors listed earlier are still important.

Stage three focuses on profitability as well as growth. The vision is well defined, profit centres are established, the organization becomes more decentralized, and the focus is on business development and market share. Problems again arise: coordination and control are difficult, service may suffer, outside factors play a greater influence, and the company may be slow to react and change. The company is larger and typically more diversified, creating more opportunities for Best people. On the downside, there may be more burnout and quality of work–life decisions that can lead to Best talent leaving. This is a critical stage in terms of the social awareness which Daniel Goleman talks about.

In a private enterprise, the owner of a stage two or stage three company may talk growth, but in many cases it's merely talk, not a passion for aggressive growth. In truth, the company coasts, fails to build infrastructure to invest and build for the future. 'Best talent' is perceptive; they understand what is happening, know where the company stands, and what that means. This can be the time of a great exodus of talent, and the company's business cycle can now be compared to the classic product lifecycle, beginning the downward trend.

Stages four and five develop formal systems for achieving greater coordination (stage four) and collaboration (stage five) with optimal use of resources. Profit sharing and stock options are common incentives for Best people. But as with other stages, problems arise, often between line and staff, and with red tape and bureaucracy. There may be great opportunities for the best talent, but now the work–life balance comes into real play. Key people don't want to travel 80 percent of their time or be relocated.

I have worked a lot with Gary Jay, an executive of Knoll Inc., one of the major US contract furniture companies. Because we have had comparable experience, both having been CEOs of smaller businesses, having worked in large corporations, and having consulted to companies large and small, he and I share similar approaches and beliefs. As we work with smaller companies that have limited slots to fill, we talk about job enrichment, how the job a talented person holds can be expanded with opportunity for personal growth and income. In larger companies, we talk about being more sensitive to work demands (such as travel and moving) that can destroy lifestyles. As Gary notes, the current workforce of Gen X and Y is not only a 'me' generation; it's a 'well-being' generation. Companies that aren't responsive to these sorts of needs can lose good talent.

Bill Kuhn

Questions to ask yourself

■ Have you personally experienced any of these talent-killers?
  - How did you feel?
  - What did you do?
  - What was the cost?
■ Have you spotted any of these talent-killers in your own organization?
  - How would you assess their impact? (H / M / L)
  - What can you do to reduce or eliminate them?
■ What can you do to ensure that these talent-killers do not emerge in the future?
■ What are the top three talent growth actions that you now propose to take?

9

Implementing a talent management system

Talent without discipline is like an octopus on roller skates. There's plenty of movement, but you never know if it's going to be forward, backwards, or sideways.

H. Jackson Brown, Jr

We cannot solve our problems with the same thinking we used when we created them.

Albert Einstein

s there a clear, comprehensive approach to managing talent in your organization? Is the identification, development and support of talent an issue at the front of senior management's brains? Is talent development something that every line manager thinks about, and more importantly, *does* something about? Everything we've talked about in the book so far points to the fact that the answers to these questions should all be 'yes', but almost all the data we've been able to uncover says that the probability of that being the case is rather slight.

A Boston Consulting Group study (*The Future of HR in Europe – Key Challenges through 2015*), reporting the results of a survey of 1,355 executives in 27 European countries, found that the top challenge facing companies is managing talent. It was also the area the executives said they were weakest in.

❝ the top challenge facing companies is managing talent ❞

One of the reasons the record of talent management is so dismal is that it is generally approached in a piecemeal fashion. Talent exists in any number of nooks and crannies across a company but if it is to be uncovered and cultivated, a comprehensive system that opens everything up is required. To use an agricultural analogy, there are two choices: plough the field under and cultivate a new one where the crop can be carefully husbanded and improved, or drain your profits away buying weedkiller.

The achievement of big tasks requires big changes in thinking, and focused action, persistence and tenacity. Without well-functioning and performance-enhancing systems, structures and processes, managers run out of interest and energy and they wander off in search of the next grail.

Start now – focus on action

An Aruspex research report entitled *The Gap Between Needing and Doing: A Survey on Why Some Companies Don't Act on Strategic Workforce Planning Needs, and How Successful Companies Do*, found that only 46 percent of the companies they surveyed were doing workforce planning of *any* kind, let alone focused talent management. Respondents reported a number of barriers to engaging workforce planning. They include things like lack of clear accountability, lack of resources, inability to quantify results, and what they term 'analysis paralysis'. Alice Snell, Vice-President of Taleo Research, says her favourite is the last one, analysis paralysis: 'It's clear that identifying the problem does not solve it. You've go to do something about it.' So when are you going to start?

Linking talent management to corporate strategy and values

In their *Harvard Business Review* article 'Make Your Company a Talent Factory', Douglas Ready and Jay Conger make the point that 'Even if a company's practices and supporting technical

> **❝talent management and corporate strategy must be joined at the hip❞**

systems are robust and up to date, talent management will fail without deep-seated commitment from senior executives.' In fact it's more than that: talent management and corporate strategy must be joined at the hip. Systems themselves will not carry the day; they need to be tightly linked to the achievement of the company's strategy and must mirror, in every respect, its vision and values. Talent management must start with the end in mind.

What will tomorrow look like? Setting the talent agenda

Momentum is the product of mass times velocity, but it's hard to create momentum when you haven't accumulated the mass, let alone trying to give it some velocity. Effective talent management must take an organization-wide approach and start at the top with the vision and values. Before any attempt is made to design systems and processes, the organization needs to nail down what it wants to become, where it wants to go, and what the enduring and essential values are that will take it there. Talent is situation specific; if you don't know where you're going, you certainly won't know who can get you there.

The most successful companies don't just have stated values; they link specific observable and measurable *behaviours* to these values. A company where the values, made explicit in what they call their Credo, determine people's behaviour is Johnson & Johnson. Alan Yu, former Managing Director of J&J Hong Kong says:

The Credo is a document that Johnson & Johnson uses throughout the organization to lay down ground rules for behaviour. Throughout the year, in a variety of locations, executives from different operating companies get together in what is called the 'Credo Challenge'. During these one-to-two day meetings, the meaning and implications of behaviour consistent with the Credo in cultural and business contexts are debated.

Research shows that companies that focus on developing a strong set of corporate values over an extended period of time, and which demonstrate these values through the behaviour of employees at all levels, outperform companies that do not by a factor of *five to six times*.

Assessing the behavioural reality of values

So assuming that an organization has an explicit and agreed strategic vision and a clearly defined set of core values, the first stage of the process is to assess the degree to which those values actually guide the behaviour of managers and staff, top to bottom. The organization needs to know where people are just paying lip-service to its values and where they're validating them by their actions.

Translating values into behaviours

Given a company's set of core values, the first step is to translate them into specific behaviours. Once you've done that, the next step is to measure how people across the organization are demonstrating the values. We do this by having every manager complete the on-line MCPI Performance Improvement Profile. The data-gathering process is quick, rarely taking more than a couple of weeks. It also provides all the data necessary for the rest of the basic stages of a talent management system. The results show who is demonstrating the organization's values as they manage their jobs, and who isn't.

Here's an example of the process. The stated values of the company in question are:

- **Transparency**: defined as involving people in decisions, being open to opinion, making the rationale for actions clear, and ensuring that all parties benefit.

- **Honesty**: defined as being sincere, providing objective performance feedback to people, treating them with dignity, and being willing to confront difficult situations openly and objectively.

■ **Engaging change**: defined as taking initiative in change, creating an atmosphere of challenge and excitement, supporting a vision, and creating acceptance.

■ **Team commitment**: defined as demonstrating strong commitment to the company's culture and values, working to overcome internal barriers, and supporting the achievements of others.

■ Accountability: defined as accepting responsibility for decisions, actions and outcomes, both individually and shared within and across teams.

Demonstrating values through behaviours

In order to be able to measure the degree to which people in the company are exhibiting these values in their day-to-day jobs, we selected five observable and measurable behaviours which the company agreed characterized each of its core values – i.e. if a manager were to do these five things, he or she would be said to be demonstrating the values. The agreed behaviours for each of the values were:

Transparency

■ Make sure the right people are consulted and involved in key decisions.

■ Make sure people see and understand what you are doing.

■ Provide clear direction for people.

■ Make it easy for people to talk to you.

■ Work for a win–win resolution to conflicts.

Honesty

■ Always treat people with respect.

■ Confront difficult decisions.

■ State views frankly.

■ Give open and frank feedback.

■ Deal with similar problems in a consistent way.

Engaging change

■ Lead change by example.

■ Drive achievement of a vision.

■ Excite people and inspire them.

■ Help people to overcome their fear of challenges.

■ Accept and promote change.

Team commitment

■ Demonstrate a strong commitment to the organization's culture.

■ Publicly praise and support individuals who model desired behaviour.

■ Look for linkages rather than boundaries between jobs, units, functions.

■ Develop strong commitment in people.

■ Strengthen the long-term relationship between employees and the organization.

Accountability

■ Accept responsibility for all outcomes.

■ Create shared commitment to what has to be done.

■ Face up to and deal with demanding situations.

■ Set a good example to others.

■ Take responsibility for your actions.

Analysis – what we are *actually* doing

The MCPI Performance Improvement Profile measures each of these behaviours on a scale of 0–10 and shows the degree to which individuals are demonstrating them. Since these behaviours are deemed to reflect the company's core values, the following type of analysis can be made.

Figure 9.1 shows the degree to which the managers in the company are demonstrating *by their observable and measurable behaviour* each of the company's core values. For instance, they exhibit the behaviours that describe 'transparency' at a level of 8.2, but 'engage change' only at a level of 6.5. (This analysis can be drilled down through the organization to show the values-driven behaviour of business units, groups, functions, levels, teams and individuals.)

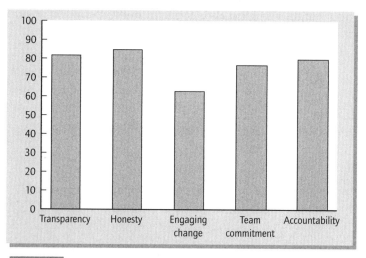

figure 9.1 Xco demonstration of core values

An organization's values are the heart of its brand promise, and employees, new recruits, customers and other stakeholders all test the reliability and genuineness of this promise every day by observing the behaviour of the organization's people. To deliver on the brand promise, it is essential that behaviour constantly reflects core values. Best is

❝ Best people need to know the organization's behaviour parameters ❞

defined not simply by the match of behaviours to the demands of the job, but by the congruence of those behaviours with the values and brand promise of the organization. You can't develop the type of talent you want unless you are clear what the underlying values of your culture are. Once you know that, you know the behaviours you need to develop, encourage and support. Best people need to know the organization's behaviour parameters.

Identifying Best and Potential Best

Having collected all the Performance Improvement Profile (PIP) data, you now also have the information you need for identifying Best and Potential Best. For each individual you have a list of the specific behaviours that they are using to drive 80 percent of the results in their job. You also have a list of the specific behaviours they think would enable them to improve their performance.

Combining these two pieces of information with the input of the individuals' managers produces behaviour specifications for every job. Comparing individuals' *current* behaviour with the behaviour specification for their job produces a measurement of Best. And comparison of individuals' *perceived performance improvement behaviour* with the behaviour specification produces a measurement of Potential Best. This process gives each individual a clear action plan for achieving performance targets.

Transforming potential into Best performance

The term 'best practice' is frequently bandied about, generally with no clear definition of what the 'best' means. The baseline reference point for so-called best practice is very rarely specified. It tends to be highly subjective and the term has become somewhat reminiscent of Samuel Johnson's definition of patriotism – the last refuge of a scoundrel. But Best performance, using the baseline of a job behaviour specification, can be clearly established. The logic flow is: situation determines behaviour, behaviour determines performance. Therefore if an individual's behaviour meets the behaviour demands of the situation, Best must result.

Potential can be defined as the gap between the behaviour required by the job and the behaviour being demonstrated by the individual. Therefore simple behaviour gap analysis produces an objective, observable and measurable action plan which, if followed, will result in Best performance.

A typical gap analysis output

Behaviour specification	Current behaviour	Behaviour gap
1 Transfer as much responsibility to people as they can manage	1 Transfer as much responsibility to people as they can manage	
2 Create integrative processes and systems	2 Create integrative processes and systems	
3 Help people develop the necessary skills for their jobs	3 Help people develop the necessary skills for their jobs	
4 Help people to learn from their mistakes	4 Help people to learn from their mistakes	
5 Make it easy for people to talk to you	5 Make it easy for people to talk to you	
6 Review and clarify people's objectives with them	6 Review and clarify people's objectives with them	
7 Set clear priorities and stick with them	7 Set clear priorities and stick with them	
8 Stress the importance of attention to detail	8 Stress the importance of attention to detail	
9 Always meet commitments	9 Always meet commitments	
10 Make sure people don't fail because of lack of appropriate resources	10 Make sure people don't fail because of lack of appropriate resources	
11 Review past performance to see what can be learned from it	11 Review past performance to see what can be learned from it	
12 Consistently track performance against targets	12 Consistently track performance against targets	
13 Set an example for delivering jobs on time, every time		■ Set an example for delivering jobs on time, every time
14 Get people to focus on how they can make their best contribution		■ Get people to focus on how they can make their best contribution
15 Face up to and deal with demanding situations		■ Face up to and deal with demanding situations

▶

Behaviour specification	Current behaviour	Behaviour gap
16 Create a sense of urgency		▨ Create a sense of urgency
17 Get people to identify and implement best practice		▨ Get people to identify and implement best practice
18 Give people frequent performance feedback		▨ Give people frequent performance feedback
19 Provide clear direction for people		▨ Provide clear direction for people
20 Make sure that procedures are helpful rather than obstructive		▨ Make sure that procedures are helpful rather than obstructive

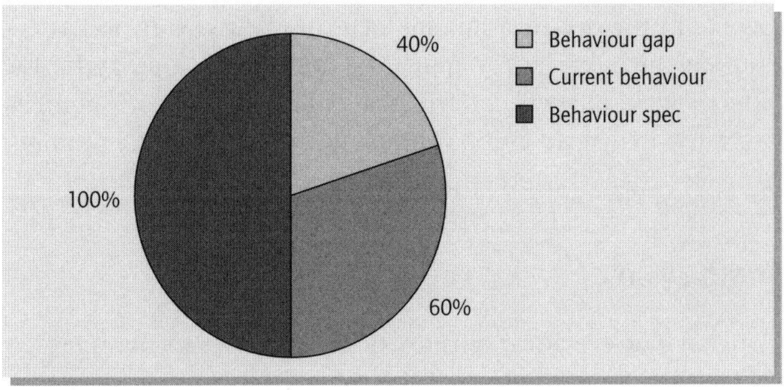

figure 9.2 A typical gap analysis summary chart

The gap between current behaviour and Best behaviour can be calculated for every individual, every team, function, division or business unit. When all the data are aggregated, a People Performance Index can be calculated for the organization. This is a measure of the degree to which people across the entire organization are performing effectively – i.e. the degree to which their behaviour matches what has been defined as Best.

Putting behaviours on to the balance sheet

Organizations have many kinds of performance and value measures – revenue, margin, profit, productivity, assets, receivables,
contracts, etc. But they don't have a measure of what they allege
is their biggest asset, their people. They declare how many
people work for them and the remuneration of the top few, but
they don't present a measure of how effective these people are.
If it's the people who drive the value then isn't it important to
have a clear definition and measure of their effectiveness? A
People Performance Index (PPI) provides that measure. Up
against the behaviour specifications for each job (*real* best practice), how well are people across the organization performing?
Are they meeting 70 percent of their required behaviours? 40
percent? 80 percent? The measurement of the degree to which
people in the organization are focusing their energy and attention on the behaviours required by their jobs is a proxy for the
effectiveness of their performance. From an investor's point of
view, the management of a company with a PPI of 8.3 promises
a much better return than a company with a PPI of 5.7.

Getting buy-in

A behaviour specification provides the answer to the question
'What does the incumbent of this job need to do to achieve their
set objectives?' If the process begins at the level of strategic organizational objectives set by the board which are then translated into
objectives for the executives, senior managers, middle managers,
etc., then managers at each level have a clear understanding not
only of what *they* need to achieve but also what needs to be
achieved by the people at the level immediately below them.

Because behaviour specifications are not produced by HR departments, but by the combined input of line managers and their
subordinates, they not only provide both parties with a clear picture of the objectives of the subordinate's job, but create buy-in
and commitment from both of them. From early in life we are
told that we must do certain things, but it's not long before we

begin to decide whether or not to follow these directives. We prefer to ignore much of the advice we are given and to learn the hard way by making our own decisions and creating our own successes and failures. We all tend to think much more highly of our own ideas than we do of the ideas of others. Therefore a key step to getting buy-in is getting input from all parties concerned.

Talent management is everyone's responsibility

Talent management is a team game. In order to win, everyone on the team has to play. Talent management isn't any particular individual's or any particular function's responsibility. Comments made by various chief executives that 'talent management is my responsibility' are really simply expressions of endorsement and support. HR should not be held responsible for talent management, but they've definitely got to be part of the team that makes it happen. Talent management is the responsibility of every manager in the organization. But equally, every individual has to take responsibility for his or her own development and career. Senior executives must ask themselves four questions:

> ❝ talent management is a team game ❞

- What do we expect from our directors and line managers?
- What do we expect from our HR people?
- What do we expect from our staff?
- And what do they expect from us?

The answer to all four is 'full commitment to getting the best out of everyone'.

Chapter summary

- Despite the logic for the need to have a consistent and systematic approach to talent management, the evidence is that it typically takes place in a piecemeal fashion.

■ What should an effective talent management system look like?

   – It should link clearly and consistently to the organization's strategy and values.

   – Values should be linked to specific observable and measurable behaviours.

   – Role-specific behaviours should be agreed for each role so that Best is transparent to all stakeholders.

   – An effective talent management strategy is continually monitoring the supply and demand requirements of the organization and adjusting its developmental activities appropriately to create the opportunity framework needed to prepare people for future challenges.

Questions to ask yourself

■ Does your organization have a 'fit-for-purpose' talent management system, as judged by the four criteria set out?

   – Does it link talent management to commercial goals?

   – Are your values tied to objective behaviours?

   – Is Best at the role level clear? Do you have a methodology to aggregate behaviours to assess how well the entire organization is doing?

   – Do you have an effective and consistent way of discussing talent supply and demand opportunities and risks?

■ In terms of implementing talent management across your organization, do you have clarity on the following four expectations?

   – What do we expect from our directors and line managers?

   – What do we expect from our HR people?

   – What do we expect from our staff?

   – What do they expect from us?

Is there really a War for Talent?

Life is a chance to make the best of ourselves. We owe it to everybody to give them that chance.

Charles Handy

Human potential, though not always apparent, is there waiting to be discovered and invited forth.

William Purkey

Our approach to identifying, creating, recruiting and retaining Best people is based on behaviour – what people *do*, and what they need to do to be Best. Dr Peter Honey's remarks, made in his foreword at the beginning of this book, bear repeating:

Everyone has a right to know what is expected of them. Spelling it out saves time, removes unhelpful ambiguity and gives people the information they need to make informed decisions about whether the behaviours that are expected of them are reasonable and in line with their value system. Describing required behaviours puts the emphasis where it should be, namely, on what it is people are required to do to perform effectively. Key processes such as recruitment and selection, appraisal and coaching, training and development, and even performance related pay, are all aligned to the required behaviours.

Best occurs when the individual's behaviour matches the behaviour demands of the job. We've shown you how to measure individuals' specific current behaviour, and how to identify

> **Best is a behaviour issue ... it's a matter of what you *do***

what they need to do differently to improve their performance. We use the MCPI technology, described in the appendix, but you may have other methods of identifying and measuring behaviour. The key point is that Best is a *behaviour* issue. You can only get to be Best at a job by doing the things the job requires. It's not a matter of your personality or of your preferences or of your star sign: it's purely a matter of what you *do*.

This final chapter is not a summary of what has been said before. There are summaries at the end of each chapter. We don't need to summarize any further. This chapter takes a step back from the detail and the specifics of identifying, developing, recruiting and retaining Best people and looks at some of the bigger issues about talent worth thinking about.

Do we have to engage in a war to find Best people?

Where is John Lennon when we need him? It seems we don't make love any more; we make war. A quick troll through Google identifies more than 55 currently ongoing, ferociously fought, 'wars' – none of them involving guns or armies. There are, of course, the well-publicized wars on terror, drugs, Aids and famine, but were you aware that there are also desperate tooth-and-nail wars being waged on plastic, file-sharing, spam, paperclips and frankincense? Or that separate wars are currently being fought against Christmas and Boxing Day? It's a wonder anyone can sleep at night with the noise of battle.

Are we out of the war zone at work? Apparently not. There are day-to-day battles over salary, bonus, promotion and status. But the great fonts of business knowledge like McKinsey, *The Economist*, and *The Wall Street Journal* say these are just a sideshow compared with the Big One, **The War for Talent**.

But wars aren't what they used to be. You used to know who the enemy was. They wore uniforms and were easily identified and defined. You also had clear targets and objectives. You knew if you were winning or losing. Now even war as a metaphor is different; it's often quite unclear what the 'war' is about, and the so-called War for Talent is a prime example. It's what Winston Churchill called a Phoney War.

Is talent rare?

There appears to be an almost universal consensus that talent is a scarce commodity and getting scarcer by the day. Among the few dissenting voices are Philip Brown and Anthony Hesketh who conducted a serious and rigorous piece of research in 2004 (*The Mismanagement of Talent*) and were able to conclude that the demand for people in high-skilled, high-wage jobs has been exaggerated. But rigorous and objective research like Brown and Hesketh's isn't taken seriously. What the organizational world has been persuaded to listen to is the largely unsubstantiated, haphazard and subjective opinion of hordes of journalists, consultants and head-hunters – the very people who invented the War for Talent and are busily exploiting their creation.

Talent is not scarce

Globalization and the rapid growth of economies such as China and India conveniently get tagged as the main forces driving the scarcity of talent. The argument is that as competition gets stiffer, as technology changes more rapidly, and as customers become more demanding, companies need more talented people, particularly managers. And we agree. What we disagree with is that talent is scarce; we believe that to be a myth. The reason the myth persists is because of a fallacious underlying assumption: that there is a finite number of talented people in the world. Ergo, when economies and businesses grow and their demand for talent grows, demand exceeds supply, and we all know what that means. Prices go up. This is a marvellous time to have a label saying *Talented* on your forehead.

But even though many accepted truths turn out to be untrue, while they are accepted they prevent people from looking outside the box, or even, in the face of evidence, *seeing* outside the box. Galileo was forced to recant his assertion that the Earth moved around the sun rather than vice versa in spite of strong supporting evidence (and the fact that Copernicus had established the fact a century earlier). More recently, in the twentieth century the same sort of fate was accorded Immanuel Velikovsky, who put forward a theory that the Earth has experienced a number of natural catastrophes which created consequences like the extinction of the dinosaurs. He argued that Earth, Venus, Jupiter and Mars were once in different orbits and relationships to one another and on the basis of his theory he correctly predicted the high surface temperature of Venus. But because he wasn't a physicist, and because his theories contradicted accepted truths, the scientific community successfully prevented publication of his articles and ideas and even forced the publisher, Macmillan, to drop plans to publish one of his books by threatening to boycott all Macmillan textbooks.

It was only after the findings of the *Mariner II* space probe proved a number of his predictions to be correct that the Chairman of the Space Board of the National Academy of Science wrote an apology to Velikovsky in which he said: 'Some of [your] predictions were said to be impossible when you made them ... I do not know of any specific prediction you made that has since proven to be false.'

It's comforting for many people to believe in a shortage of talent because they profit from it. If talented people are a rare species, then their discovery and acquisition is like finding hidden treasure. Being a spotter and recruiter of talent becomes the organizational equivalent of being Indiana Jones. It reinforces the idea that you have an exceptional ability: not only are you able to recognize talent, but you are able to attract it to your organization. And those high-priced head-hunters who help you sift through the dross in order to find the gold nuggets are not inclined to disabuse you of your delusions.

It is quite widely distributed within the population. There is no real shortage of people with ability. There are thousands of brilliant artists, thousands of singers and actors. The fact that there are relatively few 'stars' in Hollywood is not because of any shortage of acting talent. The fact that very few painters achieve fame and fortune is not because they lack talent, it's because they lack promoters. Winning the Turner Prize with an unmade bed doesn't take much artistic talent, but it does require clever promotion. Every one of the Impressionists exhibited paintings at the high-profile Vienna Biennial Exhibition. None of them ever won a prize. It wasn't talent that was lacking; it was a combination of poor promotion and an audience fixed on a view of accepted truth.

There is no shortage of talent; there's a shortage of people who understand what talent really is, where to find it and how to develop it. They fail to recognize that while one component is current knowledge and ability, the far more important element is people's potential and their ability to develop, grow, stretch themselves, learn and rise to challenges. Rousseau said it rather nicely: 'One distinguishing characteristic of man which is very specific indeed and about which there can be no dispute, is the faculty of self-improvement.' But then Rousseau died 235 years ago and perhaps human memory doesn't stretch back that far.

Can potential be identified?

Of course it can, as we have shown. But a lot of people still cling to the idea that it's a matter of having 'an eye' for it, not that there is any kind of systematic method. The authors of the book *Grow Your Own Leaders* tell of a company that created an eight-year development programme focused on individuals whom they defined as having high potential. The objective was to develop managers capable of taking on senior executive positions in the company. Over 15 years, 300 people went through the programme at a cost of more than $100 million. Only three of them made it to senior management positions!

Something is clearly wrong here. How can it take eight years to recognize that someone doesn't have the ability or potential to become a senior manager? And how can 297 people continue through the process for that period of time and fail to develop their abilities? Either the programme is deeply flawed, offering no opportunities for learning and development, or the 297 people engaging in the process understand the programme is meaningless activity, which is simply part of being a manager in the company.

The authors' explanation for the failure of the programme is 'Candidates were selected into the high-potential program because of their technical and sales skills as well as concern for their retention rather than for proven potential to grow to higher levels.' Do they really mean there was not a single individual among 297 people who had no potential to grow and develop? It's just not possible. And what do they mean by 'proven potential to grow to higher levels'? If, and it's a very large if, the company knew which people had this potential, why did they waste time with people who didn't?

And what's wrong with technical and sales skills anyway? Are sales or technically competent people doomed to the eternal limbo of lower-middle management? Do people with technical or sales skills not have potential to grow to higher levels? How about Anne Mulcahy? She started her career as a sales representative and became Chairman and CEO of Xerox. What about Jeff Bezos? He started life as a techie, doing an electrical engineering and computer science degree at university, and is now Chairman and CEO of Amazon, the world's largest bookseller. What about Marjorie Scardino, CEO of Pearson? Her first job was taking dictation at the Associated Press in Washington. And how about David Cote, CEO and Chairman of Honeywell International? He spent the first six years of his life after high school as a manual labourer. Everyone has to start somewhere and early success in a specific field or area doesn't shut the door to being successful in some other field of endeavour.

> **everyone has to start somewhere**

There are any number of suggestions and ideas about how to identify talent. The *Grow Your Own Leaders* authors think of it in organizational terms, as a nomination process. People across the organization are required to complete forms that rate people on a set of criteria deemed to describe high potential. These forms are then collected and reviewed by an Executive Resource Board. On the positive side, if a large number of people in the company put forward nominations, the resulting list will undoubtedly include people with high potential. On the negative side, unless the criteria for nomination involve things that are clearly observable and measurable, the final assessments made by the Resource Board, let alone the nominations themselves, will remain subjective. For example, some of the suggested criteria for identifying high-potential individuals include the following (our 'translation' in brackets):

■ Identifies with management – (i.e. 'reminds us of us')

■ Makes effective presentations – (i.e. 'tells us things we agree with')

■ Demonstrates interpersonal diplomacy – (i.e. 'doesn't tell us things we don't agree with')

■ Has accurate self-insight – (i.e. 'knows who to spend time with')

■ Is a good team player – (i.e. 'doesn't rock the boat')

The problem with the assessment of these criteria is that it tends to be subjective and reflects a strong sense of 'you'll know talent when you see it' – especially when, to quote Rooster Cogburn in *True Grit*, the individual to whom they are applied 'reminds me of me'.

Identifying potential: it's where you start from

The majority of systems or processes that attempt to identify potential take a trait approach. That is, they focus on a number of characteristics that are assumed to be common to people who are able to expand their skills, knowledge and abilities to engage jobs of wider scope and challenge. This comes back to the tired debate about nature versus nurture. In spite of the fact that research has shown *without the slightest shadow of doubt* that there is no set of traits common to all leaders, the leadership literature still overflows with generic descriptions of what effective leaders look like, think like and act like. It's nonsense, but it sells books, journals and, most importantly, consultancy, because the person who allegedly knows what these characteristics are holds the secret key to organizational success.

Potential for what?

In his excellent book *The Halo Effect*, Phil Rosenzweig talks about what he calls 'business delusions' – the widely held but fallacious assumptions that organizations adhere to because they appear to provide relatively simple solutions to complex problems. Talent management is one of the areas which abounds with superficial and formulaic solutions. Just as there is no set of traits that characterizes effective leaders, there is no single set of characteristics that identifies 'proven potential to grow to higher levels'. It's highly unlikely that people who knew or worked with Anne Mulcahy, Jeff Bezos, Marjorie Scardino or David Cote when they were in their early twenties would have predicted where they would end up. One of the problems that potential-identification systems tend to have is lack of clarity about the *what*: Potential to do what? Potential to achieve what? Potential to become what?

If you had lived in the same hall of residence at the University of Texas as 19-year-old Michael Dell and been asked about his potential, it's unlikely you would have said he would end up being the founder and Chairman of the second largest computer company in the world. (A story is told, probably apocryphally, that one of his high school teachers predicted that he 'would never go anywhere in life', and when she retired he saw to it that the whole school was outfitted with new Dell computers.) The fact that he was clearly intelligent and that he knew how to assemble computers would not have been sufficient evidence to persuade you to predict his career. You would have been far more likely to predict him becoming something like a successful surgeon because he was studying to become a doctor at the time.

Prediction has a dismal record of accuracy. The problem with trying to predict things is that the prediction is only as good as the assumptions that underlie it. The most common assumption is that current trends will continue. Financial regulators have done their best to counter this by forcing sellers of financial instruments to point out to potential buyers that prior performance does not necessarily predict future performance and the value of investments can go down as well as up.

A second mistake is assuming that the relationship between two phenomena will remain constant. For instance, in 1968 Paul Ehrlich published a famous book called *The Population Bomb* in which he predicted a substantial increase in the world's death rate by the year 2000 because there would not be enough food for the increased population. He was right about the population growth; the world's population doubled between 1961 and 2000. The other basic assumption he made was that the amount of land dedicated to cultivation would not increase at nearly the same rate and therefore 'hundreds of millions of people will starve to death in spite of any crash programs (to deal with the problem)'. He was partially right on this one; the amount of land under cultivation only grew by 10 percent over the period. However, he was wrong about the relationship between the amount of available agricultural land and the amount of food it could produce. Advances in farming technology resulted in food supplies per capita everywhere other than in sub-Saharan Africa growing more than 20 percent. The famines that have occurred in the last 20 years have tended not to be about a shortage of food supplies in general, but rather the logistical and political problems that prevent the food from getting to where it's needed.

Predicting potential and performance over the longer term simply doesn't work. Those who claim to have predicted the rise and success of a number of people conveniently forget to mention the number of times their other rising stars fell to earth.

Identifying potential is a step-by-step process. It's like climbing Everest. There are a number of steps and you can't skip any. First you need to get in physical shape. Then you need to learn how to climb. Then there are the various stages of the climb. You don't just start at Base Camp; you have to acclimatize yourself to the altitude. Base Camp is 17,700 ft (5,400 m) above sea level. Many teams take a month or more to walk to the base of the mountain from Kathmandu so they can gradually adapt to the altitude. After Base Camp, you establish Camp 1 at about 20,000 ft (you are already higher than the top of Kilimanjaro), Camp 2 at about 21,000 ft, Camp 3 at about 23,000 ft, Camp 4 at 26,000 ft, and finally you can have a go at the summit, 29,035 ft. (To put that height into context, bear in mind that passenger jets fly at about 30,000 ft.) It's impossible to look at someone who hasn't even completed the first step in the process and predict whether they will reach the summit.

If you think of talent identification in terms of the Everest analogy, it's clear that it's a matter of one task at a time, one challenge at a time. If you can't adjust to 17,000 ft then you won't make it to 20,000 ft, and so on. At each stage you can judge your ability (or someone else's) to reach the summit. Spotting talent and potential is about being able to see what happens at each stage of a journey.

Big hitters start as small hitters

Unfortunately, many talent identification systems focus their attention on finding people who, to use a baseball expression, are home-run hitters, who get big results quickly, who don't win the game over time, but win it suddenly and immediately, who are transformation wizards, charismatic change masters, and innovative leaders – and who make everyone, not least themselves, very, very rich. It's a wonderful picture, isn't it? Just find two or three of these people and everything will work out beautifully. It's the almost universal wish to achieve without effort.

But, applying the Everest analogy, because a person is able to hit home runs in the minor leagues doesn't mean they can do it in the major leagues. On the other hand if they *can't* hit them in lower leagues, it's certain they won't be able to do so at the top level.

Nothing in an organization is achieved without people. But while there has been no end of talk about how to account for, or assess, or value the people element in an organization, nothing concrete has been achieved. Companies still babble on about

❝❝ nothing in an organization is achieved without people ❞❞

'Our people are our most important asset' and still fail to treat that asset as valuable. A recent survey made the claim that banks are the most people-oriented organizations. The reason given was that they spent more money, as a percentage

of their costs, on people than other types of commercial enterprises. But having a high people cost doesn't necessarily make a company people-oriented. Large and highly sophisticated banks like Royal Bank of Scotland employ tens of thousands of people in their call centres in the UK, and continue to have staff turnover rates of anywhere from 25 percent to 40 percent. Costs of hiring run into the tens of millions per year.

These people don't leave their jobs because they don't want to work in a call centre; many of them move to other call centres. They move because what managers say they do in these places bears little relationship to what they actually do. A great deal of time and money is spent up front in selecting people but it doesn't appear that much effort is put into finding out what the potential of these people is, and how they can be helped to develop it. Jeff Pfeffer, the eminent academic and management consultant, says 'I don't believe that people are looking to go flitting from one job to the next. People are looking for the opportunity to have variety in their work and to tackle challenging assignments. The best companies are figuring out how their employees can have both opportunities – without leaving.'

The future – look, listen and discover talent

Why do we so strongly resist changing the way we manage people? Perhaps the word 'manage' is what gets us off on the wrong foot. It implies that the 'manager' manipulates the levers and the person who is being managed behaves accordingly. That is, of course, partially true; people do a lot of the things that their managers ask them or tell them to do. Perhaps they even do all of them. But the great blind spot in the logic of this process is what the person being managed also has to contribute.

We don't live in peasant societies any more where the skills and educational gap between the 'managerial class' and the 'working class' is massive. As much as we complain about educational standards, our societies are filled with people who have active brains, and who have all kinds of ideas about how to do things better. Don't make the mistake of confusing educational level with intelligence; the latter is widely distributed in the population. Talent is everywhere, often in the most unexpected places and in the most unexpected forms. One just has to get past one's ego and *listen* to what people have to say. And one has to understand that the vast majority of people would like the opportunity to make some sort of contribution, even if it's a very small suggestion that makes a very small difference. Tens of thousands of small suggestion that result in small changes add up to very large improvements. Toyota knows that, and for 40 years it has been listening. Why can't the rest of us?

> ❝ talent is everywhere, often in the most unexpected places ❞

Chapter summary

- ▪ The war for talent is a phoney war. Talent is not rare – it is quite widely distributed within the population.

- ▪ It's not talent that's in short supply; the shortage is in people who know how to manage it – how to identify, create, attract and retain talent.

- ▪ Can potential be identified? Yes it can but it depends where you start from. Potential to do what, to become what? This should be the starting point for any question about the identification of potential.

▦ Desire to achieve lies at the heart of talent. Potential becomes reality when someone wants to achieve something and has the opportunity and support to do so.

▦ The challenge for organizations is to create the management capability and culture to identify and grow talent.

From a different angle

Shortage of talent? Only if you can't recognize it

Scarcity of talent really is a myth and great business leaders know it. Over the years I have known and worked with many outstanding executives, and I want to talk about two here who have stood the absolute test of time – two exceptional leaders who knew how to seek out talent. They founded great companies that were innovative leaders in their industries and they identified, enlisted, and grew talent to make them run successfully. The problem is that too few leaders today spend time identifying the talent they have or identifying potential talent they can recruit.

W. A. 'Pat' Patterson

Pat Patterson was the first President and Chairman of United Airlines and the first to see that the future of commercial aviation was carrying passengers rather than mail. Shortly after graduating from Harvard Business School, I worked for and was on the board of a small company where Pat Patterson, although not a director of the company, occasionally attended board meetings. In those meetings and the social evenings that followed I began to think I learned as much from Pat as I had at Harvard.

Long before *In Search of Excellence* popularized it, Pat mastered the art of 'management by walking around'. He identified talent by constantly seeking out the opinions and suggestions of his staff. He told me once, 'I'm not very bright, but I know how to identify talent among my people, and they are the ones who have suggested almost all our creative breakthroughs.'

In stature, Pat was a small man, but he was a giant in terms of his compassion, insight and relations with his people. He talked constantly

▶

with his employees to get their ideas. Even as the company grew to a few thousand employees, he made a point to know as many names as possible. His secretary maintained an employee card file that included a small photo, company position, family data and personal interests. Pat studied these cards en route from one United city to the next (he was blessed with a photographic memory), and he touched down armed with anecdotes and personal attention to employees every time.

He mixed with his people on the runway, in terminals, hangars, airline offices, anywhere a United employee worked. He bummed cigarettes from them, called them by their first name, whether pilots, counter agents, mechanics, or baggage handlers. He talked constantly – and listened – to get their ideas. As the company grew and it became virtually impossible for him to meet the thousands of employees face to face, he launched his own question and answer column in the company's magazine, and instituted a formal recognition programme for outstanding employees.

What was the payoff? Very simply, revolutionary ideas for the airline industry gleaned from employees: the first flight attendants (originally nurses because people feared flying, later out of white smocks and into attractive uniforms because people feared nurses even more); Red Carpet Service (at first without liquor but a real red carpet); the first flight kitchen, baggage systems, operating briefing meetings. The list goes on and on.

D. J. De Pree

D. J. De Pree was the founder and first President of Herman Miller, a leading office furniture manufacturer. I've had a 25-year association with Herman Miller and its dealer network. I never knew D.J.; he was retired by the time my association with the company began, but he is a legend who looked for talent within the organization.

In Max De Pree's book, *Leadership Is An Art*, he talks about his father as a relatively young man, and about the death of a millwright in the Herman Miller factory. When the millwright died, D.J. thought he should visit the family. He went to the house and was invited into the living room. The widow asked D.J. if it would be all right to read some poetry. Naturally, he agreed. She went into another room, came back with a bound book, and read selected pieces of poetry. When she finished, D.J. commented on the beauty of the poetry and asked who wrote it. The widow replied that her husband had written it. Which raises the question: was her husband a poet who did millwright's work, or a millwright who wrote poetry? In addition to all the ratios, goals, parameters and bottom lines, it is fundamentally important that a company assess all of its people's talents and skills. Talent isn't rare; it just appears in places where we tend not to look. D.J. De Pree looked for behaviour that indicated creativity and looked for people with ideas, suggestions and who demonstrated commitment.

The De Prees established a corporate culture that identified these behaviours, with the result that in the 1980s and 1990s Herman Miller was frequently listed by *Fortune* as one of the Most Admired Companies, one of the best companies to work for, and at times as number one in terms of innovation and people management.

Great business leaders like Pat Patterson and D.J. and Max De Pree understood that the problem is not a shortage of talent, it's a shortage of people and organizations who know how to find, develop and manage talent. Today, similar examples exist. GE and others have shifted from a labour-intensive company to a thinking-intensive one. Gary Hamel, author of *Leading the Revolution*, preaches the importance of listening to new ideas. Look within your organization to where the talent lies. Assess the skills possessed by each key employee and how those skills (and people) can be best utilized. A McKinsey survey showed that only 27 percent of respondents said companies effectively match talent and opportunities. In recruiting, determine the talent you need and the best way to get it. A recent issue of *Business Week* quoted Cisco Systems' approach as being 'to hire talented but inexperienced youngsters and train them internally'. Where's the talent shortage if you do that?

Bill Kuhn

Questions to ask yourself

- What could you do to provide more opportunities to your people to achieve?
- When you look at your current organizational practice, where would you say you were strong or weak?
  - In the practice of identifying potential?
  - In the practice of developing potential?
  - In the practice of applying potential?
  - In the practice of building management capability?
  - In the area of talent management?
- What do you now propose to do?
  - What are your personal and commercial objectives?
  - Who do you need to involve?
  - What are your priorities?
  - What does success look like?

Appendix

Momentum CPI Performance Improvement Profile

Momentum CPI is a family of on-line behaviour diagnostics that focus directly on performance improvement. They provide a quick and accurate method of identifying and measuring behaviours that drive business success.

The Performance Improvement Profile (PIP) identifies and measures 400+ specific behaviours that accelerate, sustain or block performance at an individual, team and enterprise-wide level.

It identifies specific behaviours that individuals and groups are currently using to drive performance, and it also identifies the specific behaviours which will improve that performance.

Research shows that 80 percent or so of performance is driven by about 20 specific behaviours. The PIP identifies those behaviours for each individual or group.

Its focus is purely on *behaviour* and its impact on business performance. It is not a personality diagnostic. Behaviour drives performance. Behaviour is what people do, personality is about their preferences.

In every case the application and output of the PIP produces output bespoke to the individual business.

It has high validity and reliability and has been independently tested at the London School of Economics.

It has been extensively used by a number of *FTSE* 100 and *Fortune* 100 companies.

www.momentumcpi.com

Index